THE SIGNAL COMPANION

The Signal
COMPANION

•

A Classified Guide
to 25 years of
*Signal Approaches to
Children's Books*
1970 - 1994

•

Prepared by

ELAINE MOSS &

NANCY CHAMBERS

•

The THIMBLE *Press*

The Signal Companion comes from The Thimble Press,
publishers since 1970 of *Signal*,
the thrice-yearly journal devoted to books and reading
for children and young people.
Signal is produced without benefit of advertising revenue,
institutional support or state subsidy.

The Signal Companion

ISBN 0 903355 48 5 ✓

Copyright © 1996 Elaine Moss & Nancy Chambers

First published 1996 by
THE THIMBLE PRESS
Lockwood, Station Road, Woodchester
Stroud, Glos. GL5 5EQ
phone 01453 87 3716   fax 01453 87 8599

Camera-ready copy produced at The Thimble Press
Printed in Great Britain
by Short Run Press, Exeter

CONTENTS

INTRODUCTION

Signal Approaches to Children's Books has readers and contributors the world over, and welcomes thoughtful writing on any aspect of books for children and young people. Since January 1970 the journal has been published three times a year by Aidan Chambers and me as the Thimble Press.

With the approach of *Signal's* 25th anniversary in 1994, the idea of publishing a subject index to mark the occasion seemed sensible, given the increasing number of children's-literature research questions we were receiving, and Elaine Moss at once offered to investigate its practicability. She had been a Thimble Press adviser from the beginning, and her regular column for *Signal* throughout the 1970s, the period of her work on the National Book League's Children's Books of the Year Exhibition and its influential catalogue, kept her involved with the journal's development.

Soon, however, we abandoned the idea of a complete subject index to *Signal's* first twenty-five years as too unwieldy, and were supported in this view by an uncannily apt quotation (noted in an issue of the *Bookseller*) from the Preface to James Howell's *Proedria Basilike* (1664), which runs:

> *The reason why there is no table . . . added hereunto, is, that every Page in this Work is so full of Signal Remarks, that were they couched in an Index, it would make a volume as big as the Book, and so make the Postern Gate bear no proportion with the Building.*

The solution we eventually devised became *The Signal Companion*, an anthology of summaries of *Signal's* articles, grouped in broad categories and indexed. This would not only serve the needs of students and other readers but might also encourage interested newcomers to venture further into the field. Elaine wrote the annotations and I compiled the index and the cross-references.

We hope that the compact arrangement of the *Companion* will make it an efficient work of reference, and that something of the serendipity that has always been *Signal's* good fortune will affect each reader's use of it.

NANCY CHAMBERS
Editor *Signal*
June 1996

Contributors to *Signal*
January 1970 to September 1994

This listing of the *Companion* annotations is arranged alphabetically by contributor.

16

17

24

SUBJECT HEADINGS: ANNOTATIONS

ABOUT THE ANNOTATIONS

The references at the beginning of each annotation give the year, issue—J, January; M, May; S, September—and page numbers of the article concerned.

Where an entire article could have been classified under more than one heading, a cross-referencing author/title line for it is included in the relevant alternative section.

BACK ISSUES. Details of available back issues, or photo-copies of articles where issues are out of print, may be ob-tained from

THE THIMBLE PRESS
Lockwood, Station Road
Woodchester, Stroud, Glos. GL5 5EQ.

AUTHORS & WRITING

Articles by and about writers for children, post 1918; for pre-1918 writers see *History of Children's Books*, pages 75-83. The annotations are arranged alphabetically by the children's author concerned.

Dumb Bunnies: A Re-visionist Re-reading of
Watership Down LISSA PAUL
1988 M 113-22 A feminist critic's reappraisal of *Watership Down* by Richard Adams, not as an 'archetypal male-order adventure' but as a novel in which tensions between 'small-scale humane oral cultures [female] and large-scale destructive technological, literate ones [male]' are resolved in favour of the former. These concerns 'are only visible in a critical climate sensitive to the concerns of women and children.' Also discussed: anthropomorphism.

Joan Aiken JOHN ROWE TOWNSEND
1971 M 72-7 Joan Aiken, caricaturist, mimic and plot wizard, is that rarity, a lightweight writer of quality. Her novels—*The Wolves of Willoughby Chase* and its sequels—are in a class of their own, set in the realms of 'un-history', an early nineteenth century that never was.

Hope Is the Spur JOAN AIKEN
1984 S 146-51 The function of hope in the life of individuals, from Ancient Greece to the present day, and its special significance to authors—and to readers who like open-ended stories for this reason. Dido Twite in *Black Hearts in Battersea*, etc., travels hopefully, as does Felix in *Go Saddle the Sea*—and the author herself as she embarks on a new work of fiction. Also discussed: *Little Women*.

RACHEL ANDERSON *See page 13.*

Growing Pains: A Survey of Honor Arundel's Novels
CELIA BOYD
1973 J 38-51 Honor Arundel is a writer in the American tradition of Louisa M. Alcott rather than the more restricted British tradition of Angela Brazil, Noel Streatfeild and K.M. Peyton. Her novels deal realistically with sex roles, with death, with class attitudes to conservation.

GILLIAN AVERY *See page 13.*

Nina Bawden: An Author for Today ELAINE MOSS
1971 J 28-33   An analysis of Nina Bawden's skill as a storyteller, her style, dialogue, humour and realism—and an acknowledgement that into her adventure stories 'slide' social topics such as divorce or blindness or the death of a parent, while political events often provide the mainspring for the novels.

Easy Connections: **Emotional Truth and Fictional Gratification**
HUGH CRAGO
1987 J 38-62   A critic analyses his own and his daughters' responses to Liz Berry's *Easy Connections*, on the surface a teenage romance but 'true to the experience of falling in love': emotional truth refers not to daydreams (as in Sweet Valley High stories) but to deeper wishes and fears. Attention is paid to language, especially the 'stock response adjective (e.g. "beautiful") which the reader has to "fill in",' generating rapt involvement. The author applies Anne Wilson's definitions of magical and imaginative thought (see page 74) to *Easy Connections*. Also discussed: Katherine Paterson, Charles Sarland.

Blume's Adolescents: Coming of Age in Limbo
LYNNE HAMILTON
1983 M 88-95   Hamilton takes four novels by Judy Blume dealing respectively with religious pleading, with temporary disablement, with death and with physical love; she demonstrates how Blume's heroines never confront and overcome, thus growing towards adulthood, but always 'adjust and cope'. This acceptance and circularity, in a feminist age, compares badly with novels such as Gardam's for girls, Chambers's and Cormier's for boys.

Lucy Boston, Storyteller PETER HOLLINDALE
1991 J 3-6   Lucy Boston said of herself 'I am not a traveller' but she travelled in her stories in time, in space, across the boundaries of ethnology and the species. *A Stranger at Green Knowe*, said Hollindale at the service of thanksgiving for Lucy Boston, is probably the finest achievement in modern children's fiction, a view he elaborates on in 'The Darkening of the Green' (see page 117).

K.M. Briggs, Novelist ELAINE MOSS
1979 S 133-9.   In an interview, 81-year-old K.M. Briggs, author of *A Dictionary of British Folktales*, talks of the 'personnel of Fairyland' while saying she is 'not particularly psychic'. She speaks of her two novels,

Hobberdy Dick and *Kate Crackernuts*, the former helping the reader to understand the part played in the lives of seventeenth-century people by hobgoblins, etc.; the latter concerned, horrifically, with belief in witchcraft.

Writing for Children BETSY BYARS
1982 J 3-10   Betsy Byars speaks (at a Pacific Rim Conference on Children's Literature in Carlton, Victoria, in 1979) about the genesis of some of her numerous books for children and about the importance of the personal human element embedded in them. She talks too of her writing process and how the story as it develops can replace a sketchy idea of plot.

AIDAN CHAMBERS   *See page 15.*

John Christopher: Allegorical Historian JAY WILLIAMS
1971 J 18-23   Is John Christopher's Tripods trilogy science fiction or historical fiction of the future? Can historical fiction deal with the future? Perhaps we should regard Christopher's fantasies as allegories about moral choice.

How I Became a Writer KORNEI CHUKOVSKY
(translated by Avril Payman)
1971 J 3-17   A translation of Chukovsky's last radio talk a day before he died at the age of 87 in 1969. He speaks of his childhood, his early career as a journalist and translator, his worship of Chekov—and of a chance meeting with Gorky that was to change his life. In 1915 Gorky founded a children's publishing house, and Chukovsky, with his long narrative poem *Krokodil*, became a famous poet who championed fantasy in the face of Soviet attempts to discredit it. Also discussed: *From Two to Five.*

WILLIAM CORLETT   *See page 16.*

An Interview with Robert Cormier AIDAN CHAMBERS
1979 S 119-32   Robert Cormier saw himself as a novelist who wrote about young people, only discovering later that he had joined the band of Young Adult writers. He talks about the politics of power in his novels and about the difference between adult and teenage reactions to the realism of his bleak endings, the human aspects of both good and bad characters, the way his plots develop as he writes. He also discusses

the false security offered by the kind of TV violence where the good guys win, commenting that *The Chocolate War* prepares young people for the real world. Also discussed: *After the First Death, I Am the Cheese.*

Looking for a Pattern JAY WILLIAMS

1975 J 3-11   Three authors—Dorothy Crayder, Robert Newman and Jay Williams— who write for adults as well as for children discuss their motivation in writing for children and discover that 'a serious, honest writer writes for himself as well as for children'; 'I can only speak to real people,' says Jay Williams. They talk about Garner and Nesbit and Grahame and Carroll, about the resolution of problems through fantasy, and about the lack of an essential ingredient—wonder—in books specially written about social problems: Virginia Hamilton is cited as an author whose realism is shot through with wonder.

Richmal the Resilient MARY CADOGAN

1987 J 63-73   The 'William' books were really a sympathetic adult view of boyhood for adults, the boy's eye view of suburbia being highlighted by the flow of humorous episodes. The author also comments on Crompton's impeccable prose style, which is in great contrast to William's raffish speech, always represented in phonetic spelling.

JANE CURRY   *See page 17.*

Very Iffy Books: An Interview with Peter Dickinson
JAY WILLIAMS
1974 J 21-9   A wide-ranging interview with the author of detective fiction for adults and science fiction and historical novels for children. Dickinson is also a poet and speaks at length about language, about his own childhood reading, about the problems of writing dialogue for characters not his own (upper) class. Dickinson writes first, researches afterwards. He compares the American frontier myth (a wider world) with the English inheritance myth (coming home). Also discussed: Ursula Le Guin, *The Weathermonger.*

Remembering Eleanor Farjeon GRACE HOGARTH
1981 M 76-81   A personal reminiscence on the occasion of the centenary of Eleanor Farjeon's birth by her one-time editor and close friend. Also discussed: Edward Ardizzone, Children's Book Circle, Eleanor Farjeon Award, *The Little Book-Room*, Oxford University Press.

Writing 'for' Children ELEANOR FARJEON
1993 M 134-8   Advice to young writers from an author and poet published in the 1930s. You cannot write for children *en masse*, so write whatever you enjoy, never copying the old masters.

Penelope Farmer's Novels HUGH CRAGO
1975 M 81-90   With their imagery, allegorical content, mythical ingredients and paranormal excursions, the novels are not about the choice between good and evil but about the fight between chaos and control. *Emma in Winter* succeeds best in exploring this tension.

William Faulkner and Children MICK GIDLEY
1970 S 91-102   The author looks at the place of *The Wishing Tree* within the Faulkner oeuvre and expresses astonishment 'that the man whom many critics had termed decadent, even depraved, has composed a fragile fantasy, a dream of innocence'.

A Writer's Life and Landscape JANE GARDAM
1991 S 179-94   The sea, the Yorkshire and Cumbrian landscapes, sensitivity to class in childhood and a love of the theatre in her student days feed the writer Jane Gardam was to become: this essay spans many generations of her family and its influences.

Garfield's Golden Net RICHARD CAMP
1971 M 47-55   Leon Garfield's *The Drummer Boy* 'is no more a children's book than *Gulliver's Travels* is a travel book'; but the fact that this work of historical fiction had to be prepared for the children's market may be the reason it is so perfect a work of art. Comparison drawn with Thomas Hardy's *Return of the Native*.

An Interview with Alan Garner AIDAN CHAMBERS
1978 S 118-37   Persistent, perceptive questioning elicits from Alan Garner a revelation of the mainspring of his writing for children with special reference to *The Stone Book* and its sequels. Garner talks about his invalid childhood in a working-class family, his education as a classicist, which alienated him from the English novel and gave him his passion for Greek drama and use of language, and about his need to reconcile his educated self with his roots. Language is the key. He talks about the bilingualism of the educated provincial child and finally agrees that the reader created in *The Stone Book* (the interviewer's concept) reunites his two selves.

In Defence of Jan: Love and Betrayal in *The Owl Service* and *Red Shift*   VICTOR WATSON

1983 M 77-87   The author examines the role of girls in Alan Garner's teenage novels and concludes that neither Alison in *The Owl Service* nor Jan in *Red Shift* is passive (as critics have suggested) because each exercises choice, an active process. The author also touches on the class issue in defence of Roger in *The Owl Service*.

Rumer Godden: Prince of Storytellers   ELAINE MOSS

1975 M 55-60   In an interview Rumer Godden declares that self gets in the way of the novelist but that her experience of two cultures (she lived in India as a child) is reflected in the emotional strains and stresses of the characters created for her adult and children's fiction. She speaks of the differences in writing for the two audiences, of the importance of exact language, and of her use of internal dialogue.

Opening the Children's Books of the Year Exhibition

RUMER GODDEN

1976 S 15-17   Good storytelling is the most important element in children's fiction—which is why the writers of the later nineteenth century and the fairy tales have survived.

The Bare Pebble: The Novels of John Gordon

EDWARD BLISHEN

1972 M 63-73   An appreciation of John Gordon's fantasies for adolescents, *The Giant under the Snow* and *The House on the Brink*, in admiration of the 'electric charge' of Gordon's writing that 'catches a dream in words and sifts it obliquely through hard teeth'.

The Slow Art of John Gordon   EDWARD BLISHEN

1983 J 12-17   The influence of M.R. James's ghost stories on John Gordon and a study of Gordon's use of confining geometrical shapes (the Waterfall Box, for example) as metaphors for the terror of being trapped, in adolescence, between childhood and adulthood. Also discussed: *The Ghost on the Hill, The Waterfall Box*.

Rediscovering *The Little White Horse*   JOHN GOUGH

1985 S 168-75   In 1946 both Robert Graves's *The White Goddess* and Elizabeth Goudge's *The Little White Horse* were published, both stories in which the mythology of fertility, moon and sun, good and evil are vital elements. Did these books light the trail leading to the fantasies of

Alan Garner, Penelope Farmer, John Gordon?

[Kenneth Grahame]. **Reflections on** *The Wind in the Willows*
JAY WILLIAMS *See page 73.*

ERIK CHRISTIAN HAUGAARD *See page 19.*

DIANA HENDRY *See page 19.*

How You Become a Children's Writer WIM HOFMAN
(translated by Lance Salway)
1992 S 167-75 The Dutch author re-creates periods in his life in short
vivid passages—vignettes of boyhood in wartime, school ('count the
floorboards'), reading and listening, nonsense verse, being a missionary.
His message: 'Make sure you're there' in the fullest sense, always. With
illustrations by the author.

The Novels of Molly Holden ROGER ALMA
1978 J 16-24 Molly Holden's work for teenagers is 'modern' in that it
is open-ended, as is much adult fiction: it concentrates on the emotional rather than the sexual complexities of relationships.

Tarzan the Incomparable TOVE JANSSON
(translated by Patricia Crampton)
1991 J 20-24 Finland's favourite writer for children, remembers her
own childhood reading and how 'despite all the other beloved ... books
... *Tarzan* was the most important because he gave me a jungle of my
own and ... the intoxicating feeling ... of being stronger than I knew'.
The translator appends notes on the critical response to Jansson.

[W.E. Johns]. **Biggles Goes to the Cleaners**
ANTHONY E. GREAVES *See page 118.*

Dreams Must Explain Themselves URSULA LE GUIN
1976 J 3-11 Invited to write about herself and her work for an SF
magazine Le Guin claims that her work *is* herself, her characters are
'discovered', their actions arising from their being. She speaks of the
naming of place and character in *The Wizard of Earthsea* trilogy, of the
cartography, of being asked to write for teenagers and of the greater
willingness among adults in the UK (as opposed to the US) to accept
this work.

ROBERT LEESON *See page 21.*

I Remember ... ASTRID LINDGREN
(translated by Patricia Crampton)
1988 S 155-69   Vivid recollections of childhood in rural Sweden in
the early years of the century: the warm family life, the love of Nature,
and the mischief very much in evidence.

'Go On! Go On!': Janet McNeill and *The Battle of
St George Without* ELAINE MOSS
1971 S 96-101   Janet McNeill's experiences as the daughter of a Pres-
byterian minister and later as an official of the Northern Ireland
Juvenile Court, followed by marriage, motherhood and the writing of
radio scripts for the BBC, provided the human experience from which
she created the gang of Bristol kids and gained the expertise in writing
dialogue that gives the realism its edge.

Joining the Network MARGARET MAHY
1987 S 151-60   '... like our ability to use air and light, our ability to use
stories begins in childhood, and having taken them in, many of us are
then enabled to have a go at taking in everything else.' The author
describes her own childhood experience of listening to and telling
stories, her longing for fantasy and her passion, in her student days, for
Farjeon, Lewis, de la Mare, James, Tolkien, Dunsany.

ROSEMARY MANNING *See page 22.*

Rosemary Manning's *Arripay*: **Variation on a Theme**
ELAINE MOSS
1970 M 31-5   A survey of the author's work for adults as well as children and a consideration of the adventure story as historical narrative
for teenage readers.

JAN MARK *See page 22.*

Whatever Happened to Jan Mark? PETER HUNT
1980 J 11-19   The author applauds Jan Mark's first book, *Thunder and
Lightnings*, which won both the Penguin/*Guardian* competition and
the Carnegie Medal, and proposes two interpretations of her subsequent move towards the allegorical complexity of *The Ennead* and
Divide and Rule. These speculations are followed by an analysis of her

first four novels, concluding that *Thunder and Lightnings* is 'far more successful [than *Divide and Rule*] in matching the emotional and intellectual levels—to each other, as well as to the implied reader'.

Chorister Quartet CHARLES SARLAND
1975 S 107-13   Why does William Mayne, a writer of great 'subtlety and complexity' with 'an uncanny knack of seeing the world through the eyes of children', who is also an assured stylist, remain 'obstinately unread by children'? Studying the Chorister Quartet—*A Swarm in May, Choristers' Cake, Cathedral Wednesday* and *Words and Music*—Sarland concludes that while the wordplay alienates the reader from the drama of the narrative Mayne also takes the subjective viewpoint, propelling the reader into a dispassionate role.

The Mayne Game: An Experiment in Response PETER HUNT
1979 J 9-25   Hunt recognizes the polarity of opinion about William Mayne as a *children's* writer and puts his work to the test by seeking the response of a group of readers uninvolved with children and books. The questions asked and the responses elicited are described fully.
   1979 M 109-10   Maureen Crago reacts.

A.A. Milne on 'Books for Children' ELAINE MOSS
1984 M 88-92   How different (and how similar) was the children's book world in which A.A. Milne wrote his introduction to a National Book League pamphlet *Books for Children* in 1948 from the thinking about children and books in 1984 (when the pamphlet came to light)? Milne appreciates the variety of children and their catholic tastes, he is wary of the term classic, perceptive about terror and the imagination, fearful of declining standards (in an age of comics and film).

BRIAN MORSE   *See page 23.*

The Novels of Robert C. O'Brien BRIAN MORSE
1983 J 30-5   The fight against nuclear warfare and totalitarianism in O'Brien's work and why the critic believes *The Silver Crown* and the SF *Z for Zachariah* to be O'Brien's masterworks.

A Case of Commitment ANTHEA BELL
1982 M 73-81   A retrospective on the work of Katherine Paterson, including her novels set in Japan but concentrating mainly on this overtly Christian writer's deft handling of moral and religious issues in *Bridge to*

Terabithia, The Great Gilly Hopkins and *Jacob Have I Loved*. The death of Leslie in the first of these, and the period of mourning for Jess; Maime Potter as a representative of Christianity in the second; and the 'learning of charity' by the apostate Louise in the third are all manifestations of the author's Christian beliefs—evident but not obtrusive.

[Philippa Pearce]. **Tom's Midnight Garden and the Vision of Eden** NEIL PHILIP *See page 74.*

PHILIP PULLMAN *See page 25.*

Evadne Price: An Assessment SANJAY SIRCAR
1985 J 12-21 Evadne Price's 'Jane' stories (1928-47) are ahead of their time in showing adults and parents as less than godlike and girls as tomboys, a step forward from the pickles and scamps of late Victorian children's literature. But why has Richmal Crompton's William survived while Jane is in shadow?

'Origins' from *A History of Storytelling* ARTHUR RANSOME
1978 M 59-65 The first chapter of Arthur Ransome's book *A History of Storytelling* (1909) speaks of its decline as an art, traces its beginnings with early man, through the period of the sagas where man is raised higher and higher (Arthur, Charlemagne) towards the supernatural, before again returning to earth. Ransome discusses the national sagas, their relationship to one another and their literary form, regretting that the homespun stories (those of Sancho Panza) were recorded very seldom compared with the silk tales of chivalry (Don Quixote, so to speak). Also discussed: the Mabinogion, *Aucassin and Nicolette*.

[Arthur Ransome]. **Poetry and Pirates: Swallows and Amazons at Sea** VICTOR WATSON *See page 68.*

Some Thoughts on Animals in Children's Books
MARY RAYNER
1979 M 81-7 The author–illustrator of *Mr and Mrs Pig's Evening Out* takes a look at animals in folklore, fables, animal fantasies (*Watership Down, The Hobbit*) as well as in Beatrix Potter and Alison Uttley, as toys in A.A. Milne with imaginary wild animals such as the Heffalump being the source of fear, as people in *The Wind in the Willows*, and as themselves in animal books like *Tarka the Otter*. She talks about their place in story as well as about problems faced in illustration, but her

main theme is that taking the wolfishness out of wolves will only serve to distance us further from our proper exploration of the wolfishness in man.

MICHAEL ROSEN   *See page 26.*

A Book is a Book is a Book ROSEMARY MANNING
1970 S 81-90   The importance of Malcolm Saville as a writer of adventure stories for children (the Lone Pine series) and thrillers for teenagers (the Marston Baines books) that children enjoy but critics disregard. Saville's humour, the moral and social issues that are part of his plots and the oblique romance in the older series are also discussed, as is Saville's history of the life of Jesus (*Strange Story*). The author argues for pleasure reading at all ages.

Barbara Sleigh: The Voice of Magic ELAINE MOSS
1972 M 43-8   Barbara Sleigh in an interview after publication of her autobiography, *The Smell of Privet*, from which a passage on illiteracy is quoted, talks of E. Nesbit as 'the spark that lit the trail' towards her humorous stories of modern magic, regrets the word 'fairy' in fairy tales because it suggests 'spangles and silvery voices' and stresses her belief that folk tales are for everyone from nursery to university. Also discussed: BBC *Children's Hour.*

Author on the Run IVAN SOUTHALL
1973 J 14-18   Ivan Southall derives some pleasure (hearing Virginia Hamilton speak; listening to teenagers in Singapore discussing *Finn's Folly*) from a journey round the world to attend conferences on children's literature in San Francisco, Exeter and Singapore—but wonders whether exposure at such events is really good for writers?

[J.R.R. Tolkien]. Deep Down: A Thematic and Bibliographical Excursion C. STUART HANNABUSS   *See page 72.*

JOHN ROWE TOWNSEND   *See page 27.*

JILL PATON WALSH   *See page 28.*

Sven Wernström, Traditionalist and Reformer
PETER GRAVES   *See page 126.*

An Interview with Nadia Wheatley
AGNES NIEUWENHUIZEN
1991 J 35-48   A wide-ranging interview covers the political and social upheavals in Australia which have resulted in a new breed of writer (Kelleher, Gleeson, Pausacker) very different from the 1950s (Chauncy, Southall, Phipson, Spence, Wrightson). Wheatley's *Five Times Dizzy* grew from her own experience of racism; both sides of the conservation issue get an airing in *The Blooding*; and *The House That Was Eureka* gives readers the opportunity to see history also from the point of view of the oppressed. Also discussed: reviewing, childhood reading.

ROBERT WESTALL   *See page 29.*

Barbara Willard and *The Grove of Green Holly*   ELAINE MOSS
1972 J 34-9   A day spent with Barbara Willard reveals the intensity of her relationship with Ashdown Forest, Sussex, scene of her seventeenth-century novel *The Grove of Green Holly* and of *The Lark and the Laurel* and *The Sprig of Broom*, set 150 and 100 (respectively) years earlier. Her Mantlemass sequence was to fill the gap. Also discussed: reviewing.

Jay Williams 1914-1978   ROBERT NEWMAN
1978 S 112-17   An appreciation of Jay Williams, author, historian, Orientalist, humorist. 'Like Terence, nothing human was alien to him … one thing always seemed to lead to another and generally ended up in a book.' (See also page 29.)

Ursula Moray Williams and *Adventures of the Little Wooden Horse*   ELAINE MOSS
1971 M 56-61   In an interview more than thirty years after the publication of *Adventures of the Little Wooden Horse* its author comments on publishing for children in the 1930s when there were no children's departments in publishing houses but publishers like Jonathan Cape, Stanley Unwin and George Harrap took the occasional children's book with enthusiasm. She speaks of the moral qualities of the book—a fantasy in which violence, death and evil are confronted and finally overcome.

Patricia Wrightson   HUGH & MAUREEN CRAGO
1976 J 31-9   A critical survey highlights Wrightson's ease with child characters in the absence of adults, the effect of fantasy on her use of

language, her tendency towards didacticism, her strong sense of Australia past and present. *The Nargun and the Stars* is given pride of place in her varied achievement.

Re-viewing Reiner Zimnik, or 'Don't Mind Me! I'm Happy!' NINA DANISCHEWSKY

1971 S 115-25   A celebration of the sense of wonder that permeates the German author-illustrator's *Drummer of Dreams* and *The Crane*, the former a picture book for older readers about drummers 'beginning a life that is new ... marching away to a land unknown' (oblivious to the fact that the world is round); the latter an allegorical story about a crane driver who, in his isolation, witnesses the wonders as well as the follies of the world, but who nonetheless keeps his own crane in perfect working order. The Thurber-like quality of Zimnik is commented upon.

BOOKSELLING, EXHIBITIONS PROMOTION, AWARDS

The annotations are arranged chronologically by publication date in *Signal*.

The Bumpus Years ELEANOR GRAHAM

1972 S 97-108   In 1927 Eleanor Graham, knowing nothing about children's books, became a children's bookseller at Bumpus. Looking back on her experience of selling to families and the new children's departments in public libraries, she remembers visits from Eleanor Farjeon, Leslie Brooke, Arthur Ransome, the arrival of material from post-1917 Russia, Blackwell's *Joy Street* and *Jolly Books*, but gaps in poetry, information books and Bible stories. Reviewing was nonexistent in the 1920s: 'the whole question of *quality* was to occupy a few people ... from 1930 onward'. See also 'The Puffin Years' by Eleanor Graham, page 106.

Accepting the Eleanor Farjeon Award JANET HILL *See page 95.*

A Mirror in the Market Place ELAINE MOSS
1974 S 111-16   Lessons about the importance of multicultural images in books for *all* children learned on a Saturday bookstall in London's dockland, together with a report on conversations on the subject with Petronella Breinburg and Ezra Jack Keats, both of whose picture books were bestsellers on the stall.

The Children's Books of the Year Exhibition ELAINE MOSS
1975 S 114-17   A National Book League exhibition offers children, parents, teachers, authors, artists, publishers the opportunity for a cross-fertilization of ideas about children and reading.

The Other Award ANDREW MANN   *See page 115.*

The Value of Exhibitions PETER OPIE   *See page 58.*

The 'Ridiculous Risk': Dorothy Butler's Children's Bookshop ELAINE MOSS
1976 S 118-22   Dorothy Butler describes her almost bookless childhood in New Zealand in the 1920s and 1930s. She recalls the importance of *The New Zealand School Journal* with its poetry and excerpts from the classics. A chance encounter with Dorothy Neal White's *About Books for Children* fuelled her interest in and enthusiasm for children's books and led to her book agency, then a children's bookshop in the family home and finally Dorothy Butler's Children's Bookshop in Auckland.

Joyce & Court Oldmeadow: Winners of the Eleanor Farjeon Award JUDY TAYLOR   *See page 58.*

In Which Methuen Gives a Pooh Party ELAINE MOSS
1977 J 44-7   Winnie-the-Pooh's fiftieth birthday party celebrated on a rainy day in Ashdown Forest.

Accepting the Eleanor Farjeon Award ELAINE MOSS
See page 54.

Accepting the Eleanor Farjeon Award DOROTHY BUTLER
See page 93.

Stories for Life: A Book Exhibition GRACE HALLWORTH
See page 115.

The Kurt Maschler Award ELAINE MOSS
1982 M 82-7   Kurt Maschler, a publisher who had to flee from Nazi Germany, sets up an award (which becomes known as the Emil) for work in which text and illustration balance and enhance one another. In a conversation Kurt Maschler recalls life as a radical left-wing publisher in Germany where he published Erich Kästner's and Walter Trier's subversive *Emil and the Detectives* and the same team's post-Hiroshima pacifist *The Animals' Conference* (1949) and Reiner Zimnik's anti-totalitarian *The Crane* (1956).

Making Ourselves an Exhibition
GORDON DENNIS & LINDA WOODACRE
1983 M 108-11   Books recommended in the first *Signal Review of Children's Books* are displayed at Westminster College, Oxford, in an exhibition that brings insights, rewards and enthusiasm among staff and students as well as being a physical aid to book selection.

Endpapers: *Making Book Displays to Catch Readers* by Alan Heath
1985 M 128-30   Whole-school and classroom practice.

Selling the Children Short ELAINE MOSS
1985 S 135-8   The Book Marketing Council campaigns (such as Best Books for Babies) promote not the best books but the most recent books by a given author that the publisher can afford to back with heavy finance. Also discussed: Robert Browning, 'The Pied Piper of Hamelin'.

Endpapers: *A Book Chain in Action* by Elizabeth Hammill
1986 S 213-18   Account of the origins and practice of the Northern Children's Book Festival.

Ten Years of the Signal Poetry Award NANCY CHAMBERS
See page 104.

Album of an Exhibition ELAINE MOSS
1993 S 143-51   A museum in an area of North London rich in children's literature association (Hampstead and Highgate) mounts an exhibition to celebrate authors (from Leslie Brooke to Philippa

Pearce), artists (from Arthur Rackham to John Burningham) and books (from *Mary Poppins* to *The House That Sailed Away*).

CHILDHOOD READING
REMEMBERED & OBSERVED

The annotations are arranged chronologically by publication date in *Signal*.

Children's Books and the Humanities JAY WILLIAMS
1970 J 3-6   In days gone by study of the humanities was the formative influence in the childhood of those who were to become writers. Nowadays children's books influence the writer-to-be, so is it not time that a study was made of the reading-by-choice of current authors in their youth? The early reading of G.K. Chesterton, C.S. Lewis and the author described.

On the Tail of the Seductive Horse ELAINE MOSS
1976 J 27-30   The importance of subject matter as a spur to reading in the middle years. A passion for horses, for instance, can carry the young reader of *The Puffin Book of Horse Stories* into history, challenging fiction, great poetry, mythology. Also discussed: K.M. Peyton.

Cushla and Her Books DOROTHY BUTLER
1977 J 3-37   A long extract from Dorothy Butler's thesis *Cushla: A Case Study* subtitled 'Three Years of Enrichment in the Life of a Handicapped Child' describes in detail the part picture books played in Cushla's early life and the way they provided a bridge to the world. Every stage is noted in detail. A bibliography is appended. The complete thesis was published by Hodder & Stoughton in 1979.

Cushla, Carol and Rebecca VIRGINIA LOWE
1977 S 140-8   An Australian librarian who also kept a detailed analysis of her daughter Rebecca's interaction with picture books up to the age of three finds Rebecca's responses similar to Cushla's (see above); whereas Dorothy Butler believed Cushla's responses were different

from those of Dorothy Neal White's daughter Carol because Cushla was multiply handicapped, Virginia Lowe thinks the difference is accounted for by the later age (around two) that Carol was introduced to books.

Easy Connections: **Emotional Truth and Fictional Gratification** HUGH CRAGO *See page 34.*

Beginnings JOHN GORDON
1989 J 4-8 John Gordon vividly recalls his first encounter with a story in print (an advertising leaflet in a Gibbs Dentrifice pack), his father's stories and his addiction to comics—*Playbox* and *Comic Cuts* (he enjoyed the tiny pictures), then *Hotspur*, *Wizard* and *Adventure* ('columns and columns of grey print which we went for like fish after worms'). Mowgli was more wolf than Tarzan was ape, *The Water Babies* disliked but *Tom Sawyer* read and reread along with *Coral Island*, *The Three Musketeers* and other adventure stories.

Reading and Writing: The Arithmetic ELAINE MOSS
1985 J 22-6 Adult writing such as Fay Weldon's *Letters to Alice* and Maya Angelou's autobiographical *I Know Why the Caged Bird Sings* is used to illustrate Frank Smith's thesis in *Writing and the Writer*—that reading in childhood is the base from which writing springs.

Among Schoolchildren SEAMUS HEANEY
1986 J 3-16 The spirit of W.B. Yeats's poem 'Among Schoolchildren' permeates a lecture on language(s) and the education of the inner self. Seamus Heaney, the Northern Ireland poet, explores the two traditions of his linguistic identity which, he believes, should be a source of en-richment, not of division: 'the proper use of our own particular gifts', inner as well as lived experience, should be the aim of 'educators'. Also discussed: James Joyce, Sean O Riordan.

A Language for Life: A One-Day Conference Takes Stock ELAINE MOSS
1986 M 104-8 Ten years after the Bullock Report, Lord Bullock reaf-firms his belief that literature is the peak of language experience so that the school library should be overflowing not with information books but with poetry, fables and fiction. He also warns against allowing a split to develop yet again between art and science. Other speakers in-cluded teachers, a librarian, a publisher, a magazine editor.

My Mother, My Children, and Books SUSAN T. VIGUERS
1988 J 23-32 A mother, herself (as daughter of Ruth Hill Viguers) well-versed in children's literature, observes how her children 'interplay' with books, move from pictures to sequence and learn to listen *without* pictures. But the American consciousness-raising campaigns on issues of race and gender make her uncertain about classics such as *The Story about Ping* and *The Cricket in Times Square*.

Keeping Company with Wayne Booth
—and Others MARGARET MEEK
1990 M 104-13 Wayne Booth's *The Company We Keep: An Ethics of Fiction* read against the 'new obligations and challenges' of the National Curriculum and as an extension of the philosophy of *Signal*—'that it matters which company [children] keep from the time they are learning to read through the middle years' (is Roald Dahl, for all his virtuosity as a storyteller, 'good company'?) and in their teens. Books are friends. 'We now stand on the brink of discovering *from children* what they think reading is good for and how they do it and what effect it has on them' so that we can then improve our ways of selecting books for them.

Tarzan the Incomparable TOVE JANSSON *See page 39.*

Early to Read MARGARET CLARK
1991 M 112-19 Margaret Clark, whose career was to be in publishing books, looks back at her childhood reading and her love of words (Persephone, pomegranate) and attributes to this experience her faith in the written word as the most reliable form of communication.

A Childhood in Puffins WILLIAM TUCKER *See page 59.*

Reading Alone LANCE SALWAY
1992 S 153-65 A voracious reader (later to become a librarian, an editor and a translator) recalls his wandering childhood years ('Home is where your books are') during World War II and its aftermath: Ransome, Needham, Johns, and Finnemore mixed with Canning, Creasey, comics such as *Wizard* and *Beano* and the much cherished *Young Elizabethan* in which his own first review appeared. At his school reading for pleasure was actively discouraged, and seemed to be regarded 'as a particularly disgusting form of self-abuse.'

A Catholic Reader of the Thirties ISABEL QUIGLY
1993 J 5-12   In a Catholic world of the 1930s 'there was a difference between us and the Amazons outside, not just one of white socks and manners ... but of the shape and formation of our minds.' Reading included Henty and other historical fiction (even 'that gorgeous absurdity', *The Scarlet Pimpernel*), Hodgson Burnett, Streatfeild, Eve Garnett and the classics, from Shakespeare to Virginia Woolf. But *Swallows and Amazons* and *The Far-Distant Oxus* made these precocious readers feel inadequate in the face of challenge.

Pick up a Penguin AIDAN CHAMBERS
1993 J 13-27   A late starter at reading describes the revelation of hearing voices come from the printed page, his subsequent reading (*Worzel Gummidge* was seminal, followed by *Just—William*, Biggles, Ransome, etc.), and his teenage discovery of the emergent and explosive Penguin series—'elegant, democratic, unthreateningly attractive, affordable'— that changed his life. A great teacher awoke his passion for language; giving him responsibility for building the Penguin section of his school library was 'inspired teaching'. Also discussed: libraries.

Just Pretending CATHERINE BARRON
1994 S 174-6   Books are the spur for the fantasy games of two sisters in a literary family.

Little Anna and Big Anna ANNA CRAGO *See page 111.*

CHILDREN'S BOOKS IN HIGHER EDUCATION

The annotations are arranged chronologically by publication date in *Signal*.

Using the Osborne Collection Facsimiles
GABRIELLE MAUNDER
1982 J 26-37   The study of children's literature on a teacher-training course at St Mary's, Strawberry Hill, is revolutionized by the acquisition of facsimile editions of thirty-five books from the Osborne Collection of Early Children's Books. Being able to look at a whole

book instead of the reproduction of a single page, observing the friendly irregularities; a study of Caldecott as master of text and picture; a realization that the teaching of reading was already a topic for debate in the mid-nineteenth century—all these meant that the course could be redesigned to encourage deduction on the students' part (instead of simply accepting instruction).

Symbolic Outlining: The Academic Study of Children's Literature MARGARET MEEK *See page 66.*

This Way Confusion? NEIL PHILIP *See page 63.*

Teaching Children's Literature in Canada LISSA PAUL
1989 J 39-50 A report on a pre-Conference seminar at Calgary in 1988 and the writer's own experience in teaching children's literature in Vancouver, Toronto and New Brunswick: the aim is to replace, via teachers, the 'dissecting' and 'vivisection' of literature in schools with affective pleasure in reading, and reader response. The writer comments on the relatively few schools in Canada where books even supplement the ubiquitous basal readers. And she deplores the use of anthologies as a resource for teaching children's literature to students.

Escape Claws: Cover Stories on *Lolly Willowes* and *Crusoe's Daughter* LISSA PAUL *See page 68.*

Essaying the Review LISSA PAUL
1994 M 93-102 A teacher of children's literature to student teachers in Canada replaces the usual essay with a pair of exercises: the first, 'access to information', involves students in finding out about the field of children's literature and developing the ability to discriminate; the second is the writing of the 'tiny perfect review' which involves judgement, reading around the book and discovering the difference between helpful and unhelpful reviewing. Also discussed: Maurice Sendak.

Children's Books in Teacher / Higher Education
An occasional series about children's literature courses at tertiary level, by the lecturers who devise and teach them.

: The University of Birmingham W. D. EMRYS EVANS
1984 M 103-111 The best place for children's literature courses is (a)

in the undergraduate years or (b) as in-service training. The PGCE year is too crowded.

: Worcester College of Higher Education MARY CROXSON
1984 S 173-9 Children's literature as an important subject, backed up by a good library, at all levels. The Teacher-Librarian Certificate described.

: The University of Cambridge VICTOR WATSON
1985 J 27-33 Special reference to the introduction of reading schemes when the course is sufficiently advanced to discover whether these are really necessary; and multiculturalism as an organic part of the whole.

: The University of Exeter GEOFF FOX
1985 M 112-19 Special reference to a library of children's books and enthusiasm for poetry.

: Bulmershe College of Higher Education
DENNIS BUTTS & TONY WATKINS
1985 S 176-81 Author visits, a large and catholic library and the in-service MA course singled out.

: S. Martin's College Lancaster
DAVID AITKEN & ANTHONY KEARNEY
1986 J 44-5 1 An alarming ignorance of quality authors among student teachers and children.

: York University JENNIFER BAILEY & PETER HOLLINDALE
1986 S 156-71 Undergraduates in all disciplines can take a 'Modern Fiction for Children' unit. 'The principle . . . is that inert and uninspected childhood pleasure is an adult privilege which teachers cannot afford; the active conditions of childhood must include their own.'

: Craigie College of Education, Ayr ANNE SCOTT
1987 J 24-30 Need to establish fiction as essential in education in a country where fiction has long been suspect. Wide approach.

: College of Librarianship Wales, Aberystwyth
RAY LONSDALE & JOHN SPINK
1987 S 203-9 Every librarian needs to know about children and read-

ing, regardless of special interest.

: The University of Sydney GEOFF WILLIAMS
1988 M 133-41   Children's books pervasive in every course under-
taken by student teachers. Role of linguistic theory, discourse analysis.

: Armidale College of Advanced Education
BONNIE RASMUSSEN
1988 S 197-205   Aim is to induce enthusiasm for children's literature
(at all levels) by reading, writing, illustrating, using books.

**: Examining Children's Literature: Children's Books at the
University of Wales College of Cardiff** PETER HUNT
1990 M 147-58   Children's literature has been established as an integral
(but optional) part of the BA in English (not exclusively for intending
teachers). The inception of the course, its content and examination
described.

**: Children's Literature in New Zealand: New Initiatives
in Higher Education** KIRSTY COCHRANE
1991 J 25-32   An 'uncompromisingly literary' course in children's literature at the University of Waikato is being set up to combat the low
status of children's books (despite their championship by Butler,
Gilderdale, White and authors Mahy, Cowley, Duder, Gee) in New
Zealand.

CLASSROOM USE OF BOOKS

The annotations are arranged chronologically by publication date in
Signal. See also *Learning to Read* section, pages 92-5.

Accepting the Eleanor Farjeon Award ELAINE MOSS
1977 S 117-21   Newly appointed to a library post in a primary school
the speaker expresses alarm at the administrative bottleneck through
which books of quality have to pass in order to reach the majority of
children; workers in publishing, in criticism, in broadcasting are
broadly unaware of this.

The Best of Both Worlds? ROBERT LEESON
1977 S 149-54   An author who visits schools, reading and telling stories and helping children with their own stories, believes that his writing is much enriched by this experience.

'Them's for the Infants, Miss': Some Misguided Attitudes to Picture Books for the Older Reader ELAINE MOSS
See page 89.

Faces Over My Typewriter ROBERT LEESON
1979 S 151-8   Is the large amount of time the Writers in Schools project takes the author away from his desk wasted writing time, or does contact with children (who benefit from storytelling in schools and are helped in their reading and writing by it) shape the writer's own future work? Leeson takes his *Treasure Island* sequel, *Silver's Revenge*, as an example of how school visits determined its satirical burlesque style.

The Poets are Coming Today! PAT SWELL
1980 M 70-3   A report on the enthusiasm aroused by the Poets in Schools project and its benefit to teachers as well as children.

Criticism and the Teaching of Stories to Children: or How I Lost 'Paradise Lost' and Found *The Secret Garden*
JON C. STOTT   *See page 61.*

The Dream and the Reality ELAINE MOSS
1981 J 22-36   A Sidney Robbins Memorial Lecture. A children's book critic accepts the post of librarian in a London primary school and contrasts her expectations with the reality of the rough and tumble of book provision as part of a school timetable.

Return—from Tunbridge Wells ELAINE MOSS
1981 S 135-7   A group of teachers wakes up to the possibility of using picture books by Michael Foreman, Graham Oakley, Colin McNaughton, etc., with older children. The problems, as well as the advantages, discussed.

Learning Without Literature ELAINE MOSS
1982 S 169-71   At a conference in Pavia under the title *Fare Scuola in Europa* a speaker has to recast all she had planned to say about imaginative literature in school—with examples based on the British experi-

ence—when she realizes that neither fiction nor imaginative nonfiction plays any part in Italian school practice.

Endpapers *A Children's Own Book Club* by Christine Vooght
1985 J 61-2   An infant headteacher devises tactics for promoting good books.

Endpapers *A Storybook Year* by Frances Collinson
1986 S 216-18   Picture books are integral to infant classroom life.

Endpapers *Booked by Dorset* by Joan Hickmott
1988 J 73-4   An account of how one county supports literature-based learning to read.

The Historical Imagination   ELAINE MOSS
1989 S 143-55   In a tribute to the American historian Barbara Tuchman, who herself acknowledged the influence of the Lucy Fitch Perkins 'Twins' series in childhood, Elaine Moss argues the case for historical fiction as illuminator of history in school. She describes a day with teachers exploring the Cotswold setting for Cynthia Harnett's *The Wool-pack*. There follows a 'course' of historical novels that would cover British history from prehistorical times (Henry Treece's *The Dream-Time*) to World War I (Alan Garner's *Stone Book Quartet*).

Reading Classics with Young Children   LIZ WATERLAND
1989 S 187-94   A teacher whose children have been continuously drawn into reading through an abundance of the most rewarding picture books experiments with reading classic children's stories (*Winnie-the-Pooh*, *The Hobbit*, *The Secret Garden*, *Black Beauty*) to them. Too hard for six- to seven-year-olds? They had had so much book experience that they were able to cope, and to reason intelligently about relationships and motivation.

Feeding the Artist   ELAINE MOSS
1991 J 7-19   Feeding the imagination is the key to literacy in a world dominated by television and crammed with the indifferent outpouring of verse and story by publishers who try to rival TV instead of concentrating on their own special contribution—quality of word and image. The place of books in three primary schools—one with real books in every classroom, one dependent on reading schemes and one in which a teacher discovers the power of quality picture books to convert non-

readers into enthusiasts—is described.

Books and Schools: Books in Schools MICHAEL ROSEN
1993 M 103-14   A Patrick Hardy Lecture. The rise and decline of a
popular book culture in school (and out of it) in the years 1950-1992 as
experienced by the author. 1950s: few books in his primary school
other than work books; encouragement to read in a middle-class white,
academic home; 1960s grammar school: little encouragement for
leisure reading until sixth form, by which time less than 10% of the
school population was in class; 1970s: support for children's reading
from new review magazines, children's book groups, school bookshops, Children's Rights Workshop; 1980s/1990s: the beginning and
the acceleration of the decline. View of the children of the 1970s and
early 80s as the 'lost generation'. 'We [now] need to insist that reading
means cultural cross-referencing, contrasting of oppositional texts,
resourcing alternative views, and making space in classrooms for the
socialized interpretation of multiple meanings.'

Books for the First Enterers GILLIAN AVERY   *See page 82.*

COLLECTIONS & COLLECTING

The annotations are arranged chronologically by publication date in
Signal.

Amateur Joys JULIA MacRAE
1970 M 59-63   A publisher describes some nineteenth-century
treasures in her collection and ponders on their twentieth-century
descendants. Also discussed: *Robinson Crusoe* illustrations, Boutet de
Monvel, Ethel Turner's *Seven Little Australians.*

Robinsonades: The J.A. Ahlstrand Collection
MARGIT HOFFMAN
1975 M 61-74   In the Stockholm Royal Library the Ahlstrand Collection of books spawned by *Robinson Crusoe* includes an Eskimo translation and Robinsonades from all over Europe.

The Value of Exhibitions PETER OPIE

1976 J 22-6   The value to the children's books collector is to have the standard works of children's literature assembled in one place: Festival of Britain Book Exhibition, 1951; the Bussell Exhibition at the National Book League, 1946; the V&A-Opie Classic Fairy Tales Exhibition, 1975. The leap forward in the study of early children's books has led to greater knowledge of their whereabouts.

Joyce & Court Oldmeadow: Winners of the Eleanor Farjeon Award JUDY TAYLOR

1976 S 139-42   A tribute to the vision of the Oldmeadows, whose wholesaling children's book business in Melbourne, Australia, prompted them to buy a homestead in Riddell's Creek and turn it into the Dromkeen Collection of Australian Children's Literature: a refuge for authors, artists and editors; a study place for teachers and others; a centre where children come in groups 'and go away feeling that books are living things'.

Boxes of Delight: Aspects of the Renier Collection
TESSA ROSE CHESTER

1986 J 27-41   The curator of the Renier Collection at the Bethnal Green Museum of Childhood describes the immense task of cataloguing, classifying, cross-referencing and exhibiting the collection—'a closely woven intricate pattern of five centuries of child life'.

Her Clear Grey Eyes Had Never Needed Glasses
MARTIN SPENCE

1987 M 139-44   A collector of Elinor Brent-Dyer's 'Chalet School' books considers the reason these books survived the demise of the boarding-school story in the 1940s and the international aspects of the series.

The Manchester Polytechnic Library's Collection of Children's Books W.H. SHERCLIFF

1988 S 206-11   Manchester Polytechnic has, through various mergers, collected and catalogued a library of children's books and magazines from the mid nineteenth century to the present day, offering the opportunity for the study of literature, binding, typography, design and illustration.

A Childhood in Puffins WILLIAM TUCKER
1991 M 101-11 A bookseller's son describes the excitement of collecting Puffin first editions in childhood and, later, noticing the changes in editorship, the spine lettering, the numbering, the jackets, the first original Puffin—and the joy of being a founder member of Kaye Webb's Puffin Club, receiving *Puffin Post*, and setting up a Gloucestershire branch of the Puffin Club.

CRITICISM & REVIEWING

The annotations are arranged chronologically by publication date in *Signal*. This section includes *Book Post* and *Reading New Books*, pages 70-2.

Standards of Criticism for Children's Literature
JOHN ROWE TOWNSEND
1974 M 91-105 A May Hill Arbuthnot Lecture. While different kinds of assessment are valid for different (e.g. social, psychological) purposes, literary merit should be the criterion by which reviewers judge children's literature since they are not in a position to know the needs and tastes of individual children or groups. Reviews, however, tend to be child centred. The speaker takes what he describes as the 'purist' standpoint, along with Paul Heins and Brian Alderson. Literary experience is therefore the prerequisite for a reviewer (or *Guardian* Award judge), the critic counting for more than the criteria. Also discussed: Matthew Arnold, T.S. Eliot.

Criticism and Children's Literature PETER HUNT
1974 S 117-30 Children's books that rank as literature (defined) can and should be subjected to literary criticism of the same depth as criticism of adult literature: 1. Factual study including the contextual approach; 2. Objective process (use of language, etc.); 3. The critic's subjective response. 'Whatever critical theory we produce for children's literature it will have little or nothing to do with children.' Reference is made to Brian Alderson and John Rowe Townsend, with whose views the writer broadly concurs.

To the Toyland Frontier ROBERT LEESON
1975 J 18-25 The children's books reviews editor of the *Morning Star* welcomes the change 'from minority interest to something like a mass movement' in children's literature and challenges the 'purist' critics to abandon their solely literary criteria and embrace 'the new universality'. Also discussed: Brian Alderson, John Rowe Townsend.

Chorister Quartet CHARLES SARLAND *See page 41.*

Critical Method for Children's Literature: A Booklist
PETER HUNT
1976 J 12-21 An annotated bibliography of works about criticism for the children's book person who may not have encountered the principles and the terminology.

Pig-in-the-Middle: Some Reflections on the Function of the Children's Book Reviewer ELAINE MOSS
1977 M 59-63 The 'purist' critic and the 'pragmatic' reviewer who takes the child reader into account are both part of the same drive: to bring the worthwhile book to the receptive reader. Reviewing in national newspapers is the place for pragmatism with criticism finding its home in specialist journals.

The Reader in the Book: Notes from Work in Progress
AIDAN CHAMBERS
1977 M 64-87 An analysis of the main tenets of modern critical theory (Wolfgang Iser, Wayne C. Booth) demonstrates the important role of the reader as a formative partner in the writer's work. This being so, children's literature can be judged by the same criteria as adult literature, the child being taken into consideration as 'the reader in the book'. Aidan Chambers compares Roald Dahl's style when writing for adults with that when writing for children; he proceeds to a detailed examination of Lucy Boston's *The Children of Green Knowe* and its implied reader. (Recipient of the first Children's Literature Association Award for critical writing.)

The Cool Web reviewed by C.S. HANNABUSS
1977 M 88-90 A review of *The Cool Web: The Pattern of Children's Reading* (edited by Margaret Meek, Aidan Warlow and Griselda Barton) highlights its nature as a critical synthesis drawn from many disciplines and suggests it as a blueprint for those involved in the field in the future.

The Mayne Game PETER HUNT *See page 41.*

Cultural Categories and the Criticism of Children's Literature HUGH CRAGO

1979 S 140-50   The assumption that children's response to literature is different from that of adults stems from a false comparison of children-in-general not with adults-in-general but with literary articulate adults. The critic of children's books, learning from psychoanalysis, should project his/her personal response to children's literature rather than a distanced third-person view because individual response is what gives life to art. Reference made to the work of Edmund Leach.

Questions of Response MARGARET MEEK

1980 J 29-35   A teacher of teachers who also reviews children's books analyses her ways of reading submissions under three headings, which are then expanded. 1. Her engagement with the book as a whole; 2. The subjective questions she asks ('Was I bored?' 'On whose behalf am I reading?' etc.); 3. The objective assessments she makes (e.g. author's stance; rhetorical patterning; literary conventions). An annotated list of works on 'the act and art of reading' is appended.

Criticism and the Teaching of Stories to Children: or How I Lost 'Paradise Lost' and Found *The Secret Garden* JON C. STOTT

1980 M 81-92   An academic applies his techniques of criticism first to children's literature, then to a carefully prepared progression of picture books and stories in a classroom of six- to seven-year-olds: he discovers, using the enclosed world of the garden as his pivot, that enjoyment of books is progressive and that children as young as six can discern pattern and story structure. Also discussed: Leslie Brooke, F.H. Burnett, Beatrix Potter.

Coming to Books MARGERY FISHER

1980 S 127-9   The editor/proprietor of the review journal *Growing Point* approaches reviewing first by reading the book for enjoyment, then rereading to bring critical response born of training and experience to bear. 'Children must learn to come towards the book, not the other way round.'

Criticism and Pseudo-Criticism PETER HUNT

1981 J 14-21   In reviewing David Rees's *The Marble in the Water: Essays on Contemporary Writers of Fiction for Children*, Peter Hunt deplores soft-centredness and pseudo-criticism in this field and maintains that the study of children's books *is* a discipline. He expands on the theme, rejecting a critic's right to be prescriptive.

Re-viewing Reviews STUART HANNABUSS
1981 M 96-107   A thoroughgoing survey of the reviewing of children's books. Who is it for?, what is its purpose?, local and national publications, the long critique, the short review, reviews of critical works, the special problem of reviewing picture books, and the review *à thèse* in places like *Spare Rib*. The conclusion: we need horses for courses and, as a reviewer, 'you have to aim at being everything to other people, yet still remain very much yourself'.

Taking a Good Look at Picture Books CELIA BERRIDGE
1981 S 152-8   Deploring the way picture books are treated by reviewers (short reviews, often reflecting only one aspect of the work, with too much concentration on text and not enough on the visual aspect), Celia Berridge provides a long review of Janet and Allan Ahlberg's *Each Peach Pear Plum* as an example of the respect which this money-spinning branch of the book trade deserves.

A Fine Scepticism: Academics, Children and Books
PETER HUNT
1981 S 175-81   Reviewing Neil Philip's *A Fine Anger: A Critical Introduction to the Work of Alan Garner* and Nicholas Tucker's *The Child and the Book: A Psychological and Literary Exploration*, Peter Hunt sets the enthusiasm and detail of Philip beside the tentative findings of Tucker. They exist, he says, in an 'ambiguous' world in which academia must find the sharp edge combined with accessibility at present lacking.

False Premises CHARLES SARLAND
1982 J 11-20   Reviewing Fred Inglis's *The Promise of Happiness: Value and Meaning in Children's Fiction*, Sarland finds himself out of sympathy with Inglis's philosophical stance (an apparent desire for the re-establishment of the values of the 'cultivated property-owners of Victorian England') and dissatisfied with Inglis's attempt to apply Leavisite principles to children's fiction. He challenges the assertion that the great children's novelists are Carroll, Kipling, Burnett, Ransome, Mayne and Pearce (Sarland would add others, believing that historical texts should have something to offer today's readers); in Sarland's view Inglis also

fails to give the texts the close attention of his Leavis model.

The Readers in the Reader: An Experiment in Personal Response and Literary Criticism   HUGH CRAGO

1982 S 172-82   Hugh Crago tests his theory (see page 61) by reading Jill Paton Walsh's *A Chance Child* and making notes (full at the beginning, slighter towards the end as the novel takes over) about his responses. These he analyses as (a) awareness of an emotional defence against involvement in an unfamiliar situation; (b) rational activity to distance himself from the novel; and (c) a synthesizing critical mode. Only (c) is an adult response. Is criticism therefore 'a defence against disquieting emotional reactions to a work of art'?

The Writers in the Writer: A Reply to Hugh Crago
JILL PATON WALSH

1983 J 3-11   Jill Paton Walsh appreciates Hugh Crago's analysis of his reactions while reading *A Chance Child*, some of which mirror her own emotions at the time of writing. She believes, though, that the reading axis is not purely author/reader but that the subject written/read about makes the transaction three-way, enlarging the reader's experience.

The Child's Changing Story   AIDAN CHAMBERS

1983 J 36-52   In a changing world Story (which reflects, finds, creates meanings in relation to the world we live in) must also be changing. Five important changes in the twentieth century are: the General Theory of Relativity; the conquest of space; attitudes to gender; nuclear fission; and television. Developments in children's books are related to these changes. Also discussed: Raymond Briggs, Anthony Browne, Robert Cormier, Alan Garner's *The Stone Book*, Felice Holman's *Slake's Limbo*, Gene Kemp's *The Turbulent Term of Tyke Tiler*.

Talking Pictures: A New Look at *Hansel and Gretel*
JANE DOONAN   *See page 85.*

The Secret Seven versus *The Twits*: Cultural Clash or Cosy Combination?   CHARLES SARLAND   *See page 116.*

This Way Confusion?   NEIL PHILIP

1984 J 12-18   In a review article about Robert Bator's *Signposts to Criticism of Children's Literature* Neil Philip gives an overview of the approaches to the task of the critics represented while adding his own observations. 'The critic must be a reader first . . . How can one say anything interesting or illuminating about a book one has not read as it was supposed to be read: that is, in the open, unhurried expectation of pleasure'; 'Criticism of children's literature cannot afford to keep one eye on the text and the other on university English departments.'

Childist Criticism: The Subculture of the Child, the Book and the Critic PETER HUNT

1984 J 42-59   Is there a counter-culture through childhood which produces a child's way of reading which is essentially different from that of the adult? The author examines schools of criticism in the adult field and critics of children's literature who embrace their theories. He concludes that 'the one thing we should avoid is the assumption that an adultist reading is the only one possible, that children as well as adults recognize literary merit (their perceptions seem likely to be different, but they will only seem to be inferior if we play the game that way)'; and that childist criticism isn't the whole answer, merely a useful contribution to understanding the split between, for example, the work of Hugh Crago and that of John Rowe Townsend, childist and adultist respectively.

1984 M 120-2   John Rowe Townsend comments.

Two Artists Telling Tales: Chihiro Iwasaki and Lisbeth Zwerger   JANE DOONAN   *See page 87.*

Speaking of Shifters   MARGARET MEEK

1984 S 152-67   Time in stories and stories in time: an analysis of 'shifters' in the language of stories (e.g. the past tense) told by children as they grapple with the concept of time—and by great storytellers such as William Mayne, Maurice Sendak, Alan Garner ('a fine counterpointing of historical time and the existential now' in *The Stone Book Quartet*) but principally Philippa Pearce. Margaret Meek makes a detailed study of time in *Tom's Midnight Garden* and compares it with the part played by past, present and future in the deceptively straightforward narrative in *The Way to Sattin Shore*.

Questions of Method and Methods of Questioning: Childist Criticism in Action   PETER HUNT

1984 S 180-200   There are many possible readings of any text depending on the age, the personality, the experience of the reader and his/her purpose in reading. Children read differently from adults so, if we want

to say something worth saying rather than reproducing inappropriate critical gestures, 'we must consider "possible" and "probable" readings in place of "adultist" readings'. There follows an analysis of Betsy Byars's *The Eighteenth Emergency* from a childist critical viewpoint.
1985 J 61-6   Victor Watson's objections; PH replies; VW responds.

Tony Ross: Art to Enchant JANE DOONAN *See page 87.*

The Black Rabbit JOHN GOLDTHWAITE
1985 M,S 86-111, 148-67   A two-part analysis (part 1, overview; part 2, detailed) of the importance of the publication in 1880 of Joel Chandler Harris's *Uncle Remus: His Songs and Sayings.* The oral culture of the American Negro there faithfully recorded gave rise, through Brer Rabbit and other characters, to the evolution of the old beast fable into twentieth-century anthropomorphic prose fantasy (*The Tale of Peter Rabbit, The Wind in the Willows, The Just-So Stories, Old Mother West Wind*) and, later, Babar and Mickey Mouse. A seminal book in the history of children's literature (comparable to Grimm or the Arabian Nights) it became nevertheless a target for the US civil rights movement in the 1960s. The Uncle Remus stories, as evident in the conundrum of Mz Meadows, were trickster stories for the whole community, not bedtime stories for children.

Inside the Lurking-glass with Ted Hughes LISSA PAUL
See page 100.

Outside Over There: **A Journey in Style** JANE DOONAN
See page 88.

A Signal Conversation HUGH CRAGO
1986 M 122-40   On the occasion of *Signal's* fiftieth issue, a regular contributor 'charts the history of some ideas about children and their reading matter as they have been explored in the pages of *Signal* over the past decade', citing articles by Robert Leeson, Elaine Moss, John Rowe Townsend, Peter Hunt, Dorothy Butler, Aidan Chambers, Virginia Lowe, Lance Salway, Anne Wilson, Jane Doonan, Jill Paton Walsh, Charles Sarland.

Easy Connections... HUGH CRAGO *See page 34.*

Sis Beatrix JOHN GOLDTHWAITE *See page 78.*

Symbolic Outlining: The Academic Study of Children's Literature MARGARET MEEK
1987 M 97-115 'The academic study of children's literature cannot sit within one specialist discipline. It needs a social and intellectual space where a set of collaborative possibilities can be worked out ... the disregarded history of children's books is that which is locked into each reader. We all bring to each new book the history of all we have read.' Margaret Meek's plea is for a greater understanding of the learning-to-read process and of the meaning children extract from every variety of verbal experience—the social nature of reading that is not taken into account in psychological studies. 'Texts of multiple meanings [which include the picture books of Burningham and Sendak] offer the reader the chance to discover fiction as the focus of the contemplation of *possibilities*: what life might be like.'

Enigma Variations: What Feminist Theory Knows about Children's Literature LISSA PAUL
1987 S 186-202 Having analysed the difference between male discourse on literature (laying bare the text) and female ('keeping the voyeur's attention engaged while the clothes are being taken off') the author sets out to show that as others (i.e. women and children) begin to enjoy freedom as people, feminist critics and critics of children's literature must learn to accord value to 'otherness'. She compares Burnett's *The Secret Garden* (in which Mary makes the running but Colin reaps the reward) with Mahy's *The Changeover*, in which Laura is the brave and resourceful heroine while the boy Sorry keeps watch. References made to the work of Humphrey Carpenter, Peter Brooks, Northrop Frye, among others. A recommended reading list of relevant critical work is appended.

Ideology and the Children's Book PETER HOLLINDALE
See page 116.

Dumb Bunnies LISSA PAUL *See page 33.*

The Idle Bear and the Active Reader JANE DOONAN
See page 86.

What Do We Lose When We Lose Allusion?: Experience and Understanding Stories PETER HUNT
1988 S 212-22 In an attempt to see a passage—from *Isaac Campion* by

Janni Howker—in the way a new reader, unaware of the significance of the allusions made, would approach it, Peter Hunt sets out to identify sources of puzzlement. Language (and dialect), historical knowledge, intertextual reference all play their part in mystifying the inexperienced. If we know how these 'meshes' are made we can help the 'outsider' to become an 'insider'.

Realism and Surrealism in Wonderland: John Tenniel and Anthony Browne JANE DOONAN *See page 85.*

Intimations of Imitations: Mimesis, Fractal Geometry and Children's Literature LISSA PAUL
1989 M 128-37   Some modern philosophical concepts in the fields of language (mimesis) and geometry seen as relevant to story and the picturing of story: both concepts allow for recognition of multiplicity, variety and irregularity in the repetition of self-similar patterns—just as children do when hearing a story again and again. Also discussed: Ted Hughes, *What Is the Truth?*

Invisible Pictures PHILIP PULLMAN
1989 S 160-86   An analysis of the relationship of word and image. From Caxton, via the emblem book, the penny dreadful, the illustrated novel, to Rupert Bear there exists a hierarchy in which print takes precedence over picture. With the advent of comic strip the possibility of counterpoint ('the greatest storytelling discovery of the twentieth century') arrives. This is part of the same development in film and television, and heralds the graphic novel (e.g. *Watchmen* by Alan Moore and Dave Gibbons), for which picture books by Sendak and Burningham have prepared us. The effect of film and TV on children's writing: they tend to write dialogue only.

The Constructedness of Texts: Picture Books and the Metafictive DAVID LEWIS
1990 M 131-46   Post-modernism, the picture book and picture-book criticism: David Lewis defines the metafictive in fiction, then demonstrates its features—boundary-breaking, excess and indeterminacy—in picture books. For example, boundary-breaking in Hoban and Blake's *Monsters*; excess in Murphy's *On the Way Home*; indeterminacy in Burningham's *Granpa*. He describes contemporary reviewing of picture books (pedagogic or aesthetic or literary) and suggests that recognition of the picture book's flexibility and fluidity as a 'bifurcated art

form' is overdue. Reference made to Mikhail Bakhtin, *The Dialogic Imagination*.

Escape Claws: Cover Stories on *Lolly Willowes*
and *Crusoe's Daughter* LISSA PAUL
1990 S 206-20 Although Robinsonades are considered to be 'children's fiction', two, by women about women exiled to the desert island of an ordered home life, are published for adults—though their covers have a childlike quality. Sylvia Townsend Warner's *Lolly Willowes* has witches on broomsticks, Jane Gardam's *Crusoe's Daughter* shows a young girl in front of a yellow house. A feminist critic who teaches children's literature uses these texts to explore the 'politics of exclusion' (women writers, writers for children), the politics of imperialism (rejected by both heroines, who choose to remain single) and the language of silence. These subversive texts, used in class, disrupt the value system of superiority that most students bring to the study of children's literature.

The Critic and the Child PETER HOLLINDALE
1991 M 87-100 Reviewing three volumes on children's literature (Higonnet & Rosen, editors, *Children's Literature* Volume 18; *Travellers in Time: Past, Present and To Come*; Peter Hunt, editor, *Children's Literature: The Development of Criticism*) gives Hollindale the opportunity to formulate his own views. Children's literature provides 'rich . . . opportunities both for intelligent developmental critiques and for tendentious rubbish, for being useful and for being worse than useless' to those at the sharp end where the children are. He cites Margaret Meek as the 'trail-blazer of critical activity on behalf of children'; and he defends *The Velveteen Rabbit* against Kleinian interpretation.

Poetry and Pirates: Swallows and Amazons at Sea
VICTOR WATSON
1991 S 154-64 There is no great tradition of children's literature from Lewis Carroll to Philippa Pearce—just a series of fresh starts, of which *Swallows and Amazons* was one. Ransome enmeshes his readers in a whole rich culture, not just a children's culture; his characters do not develop; they are magical characters 'who go adventuring into our imaginative lives'. *Missee Lee* is likened to oral storytelling, and storytelling, with its dependence not merely on narrative but on cultural recognition, is discussed. Also discussed: *Peter Duck*.

Do You Admire the View?: The Critics Go Looking for Nonsense JOHN GOLDTHWAITE

1992 J 41-66 Spurred on by two critics—Elizabeth Sewell, who avers that Nonsense rules out the elements of real life, and Humphrey Carpenter, who agrees and believes with Lear that it must end in Nothing—Goldthwaite examines the *Alice* books in general and 'The Walrus and the Carpenter' in particular in order to show that Carroll was not a closet atheist but an author whose 'lessons about lessons' were for life. His was a logical literary nonsense (as opposed to the fanciful populist nonsense of, say, 'Ten Little Injuns') with a moral register. The history of nonsense from folk tale to Catherine Sinclair, Charles Kingsley and Dr Seuss is traced. The reprogramming of nonsense into Nonsense so that it joins the canon of modernist thought is not approved.

Views on Reviews and Views from the Balcony HEATHER SCUTTER

1993 S 184-201 A national conference on reviewing in Adelaide, Australia, heard Heather Scutter compare the treatment in review columns of adult books (plenty of space, wide representation of reviewers, negative as well as positive) with that given to children's (fixed nominated reviewers, little space, packages of books reviewed together, no room for contextualization or evaluative commentary, mainly positive). 'Children and their fiction are part of the larger culture, not a pastoral niche.' She calls for 'a greater awareness of cultural and discourse theory, of feminist and childist theory in terms which engage with whoever the oppressors are'.

Rupert in Space and Time HUGH CRAGO

1994 J 3-16 The Rupert cartoon strip in the Bestall years seen as a manifestation of Piaget's pre-operational level of development, as a carrier of the political message of benevolent despotism and as a reflection of technological changes in the world outside: the later Rupert travels from the safety of home, through the transitional space of Nutwood Common and into his fantasy adventures not on a magic carpet but via new technological inventions. Comparisons are drawn with Blyton's Faraway Tree stories; also with Diana Wynne Jones's *Archer's Goon* and other adventure stories featuring 'non-specific inventions'.

Views on Reviews: A Patchwork NANCY CHAMBERS

1994 J 37-47 The keynote presentation at the Australian reviewing conference mentioned above centred on the following motifs. 1. The book as standpoint. 2. The creative combination of the diffuse experience of specialist reviewers. 3. The speaker's experience of editing different kinds of written discourse in the USA and UK. 4. An amendment to a 1982 view of critics: children's responses in the intervening decade have become central to adult discussion of children's literature. At the same conference JENNY PAUSACKER describes how the Children's Book Writers' Group in Australia surveys the reviewing of children's books.

These Piglets Fled Away PETER HOLLINDALE *See page 81.*

Into the Dangerous World: *We Are All in the Dumps with Jack and Guy* by Maurice Sendak JANE DOONAN *See page 88.*

Book Post LANCE SALWAY & NANCY CHAMBERS
Between 1977 and 1982 *Signal* initiated an experiment in collaborative reviewing. This took the form of a running correspondence between Lance Salway and Nancy Chambers (Book Post) with subsequent comments from readers (Book Post Returns).

1977 M 91-106   Nature of reviewing; teenage reading; differences US/UK; Virginia Hamilton's *Arilla Sundown.*
1977 S 155-68   **Book Post Returns** from publishers Marni Hodgkin and Margaret Clark and from librarian Phyllis Parrott, on teenage fiction.   **Book Post**: John Goldthwaite; picture books; Jeannie Baker's *Grandfather,* Raymond Briggs's *Fungus the Bogeyman*; Brian Alderson's *Looking at Picture Books.*
1978 J 34-55   **Book Post Returns** from Dorothy Butler (*Potter Brownware, From Morn to Midnight,* Cushla, *Grandfather, Bird, A Walk in the Park, Benjamin and Tulip,* picture-book reviewing); from Richard Barlow (teenage fiction); from Jay Williams (John Goldthwaite). **Book Post**: Penelope Farmer's *Year King*; Helen Cresswell's *Ordinary Jack*; Angela Bull's *Griselda*; teenage books.
1978 M 92-107   **Book Post Returns** from John Rowe Townsend; from Penelope Farmer (*Year King,* young-adult fiction, *Red Shift*). **Book Post**: Robert Lawson's *Rabbit Hill*; *Moffatt's Road,* Simon Watson's *Hobbledehoy,* differences US/UK, Penelope Lively's *Voyage of QV66, My Naughty Little Sister,* teenage reading, Paul Zindel's *Confessions of a Teenage Baboon.*

1979 J 54-8   **Book Post Returns** from Jessica Yates (*Year King*, young-adult books).

1979 M 110-13   **Book Post:** Paul Zindel, *The Undertaker's Gone Bananas*, Barbara Wersba, *Tunes for a Small Harmonica,* William Mayne, *While the Bells Ring.*

1979 S 171-6   **Book Post:** Judy Blume, Katherine Paterson, Rosa Guy, Robert Cormier, *After the First Death*; differences US/UK; *Exeter Blitz, Conrad's War*, Carnegie Medal.

1980 J 57   Letter from David Rees (on *Exeter Blitz*, Carnegie Medal). **Book Post:** awards, 'message books', Toeckey Jones, *Go Well, Stay Well.*

1980 M 114-15   Letter from Cecilia Gordon (*Exeter Blitz*, David Rees); letter from chair of Carnegie Selection Committee. **Book Post:** *The Light of Day*, Betsy Byars's *Night Swimmers*, Paul Zindel's *A Star for the Latecomer*, Dorothy Butler's *Babies Need Books*; 'message books'.

1980 S 177-80   Brian Alderson; Margaret Nancy Cutt, *Ministering Angels, Grandfather.*

1981 J 60   Letter from Brian Alderson.

1982 J 52-7   The final instalment of **Book Post.**

From 1982 to 1990 new books were collaboratively reviewed in annual surveys published by the Thimble Press: *The Signal Review of Children's Books 1* and *2* (covering 1982 and 1983) and *The Signal Selection of Children's Books 1984, 1985, 1986, 1987, 1988, 1989.* In 1991 new-book coverage reverted to the pages of *Signal* in an occasional *Reading New Books* feature.

Reading New Books

1991 J 49-66   Jane Doonan writes about two picture books, *The True Story of the 3 Little Pigs!* and *A Boy Wants a Dinosaur*, and responds to Nancy Chambers's questions about her writing. Elizabeth Hammill writes about a teenage book, *Daughter of the Wind*, and Margaret Clark suggests what readers may be finding in books like it. Mary Steele writes about Rosemary Sutcliff's *The Shining Company* and Jan Mark's *Finders, Losers.*

1991 M 129-42   Jane Doonan and David Lewis correspond about picture books; Jane writes about two visualizations of Aesop, David about his pick of 1990's paperback picture books, concentrating on Quentin Blake's *Mrs Armitage on Wheels.* They then comment on the difference between their approaches.

1991 S 198-213   Mary Steele recommends over thirty additional titles as an update to her Signal Bookguide, *Traditional Tales*. Elizabeth Hammill responds to the picture-book discussion between Jane Doonan and David Lewis, emphasizing the appeal of *Mrs Armitage on Wheels*.

1992 J 67-74   Elizabeth Hammill surveys current series publishing for six- to nine-year-olds; she and Nancy Chambers exchange views; she recommends Richard Tulloch's *The Brown Felt Hat* and Martin Waddell's *Little Obie and the Big Flood*.

1992 M 138-42   Pauline Thomas writes about teenage books. See page 120.

1993 S 202-5   Roberto Piumini's *Mattie and Grandpa* reviewed by several hands. See page 129.

FANTASY

The annotations are arranged chronologically by publication date in *Signal*.

On the Elvish Craft JANE CURRY
1970 M 42-9   Fantasy, the traditional imagined narrative of action (e.g. Mary Norton's *The Borrowers*), is compared with phantasy defined by Curry as a whole built up around a theme, person, place or relationship (e.g. Alan Garner's *The Owl Service*). Few novels fall entirely into one category or the other (e.g. Kenneth Grahame's *The Wind in the Willows*) but generally speaking 'Whimsical fantasy may give us deep delight, but "visionary" fantasy [phantasy] can give us joy'.

Ursula Moray Williams and *Adventures of the Little Wooden Horse* ELAINE MOSS   *See page 44.*

John Christopher: Allegorical Historian JAY WILLIAMS
See page 35.

Deep Down: A Thematic and Bibliographical Excursion
C. STUART HANNABUSS
1971 S 87-95   Tolkien's *Lord of the Rings* has 'vindicated the fantasy

tradition from the criticism that the genre is a mere "contamination of reality by dream".' The dream becomes reality, as in Pearce, Garner, Boston, Alain-Fournier and Mayne. The centrality of its insights into the human condition and spiritual potential are appraised while the many misinterpretations (the occult, the political) are questioned.

Re-viewing Reiner Zimnik, or 'Don't Mind Me! I'm Happy!' NINA DANISCHEWSKY *See page 45.*

Barbara Sleigh: The Voice of Magic ELAINE MOSS *See page 43.*

A World Beneath the Waves: The Imagery of the Underwater Otherworld in Children's Fiction 1840-1971 HUGH & MAUREEN CRAGO
1973 M,S 74-87, 123-34   The undersea world as used in children's stories from Charles Kingsley's *The Water Babies* to Lucy Boston's *The Sea Egg* is explored for its physical description, its metaphysical content, its symbolism, its iconography, its folk-tale aspects and its attempts at 'reality'.

Dreams Must Explain Themselves URSULA LE GUIN *See page 39.*

Penelope Farmer's Novels HUGH CRAGO *See page 37.*

Patricia Wrightson HUGH & MAUREEN CRAGO *See page 44.*

Modern Fantasy: Five Studies reviewed by HUGH CRAGO
1976 M 64-7   A review of C.N. Manlove's book concludes that although the works studied are in the main for adults, the book has much to offer those interested in fantasy for children.

Reflections on *The Wind in the Willows* JAY WILLIAMS
1976 S 103-7   Jay Williams chooses *The Wind in the Willows* as the most interesting piece of writing for children from a technical standpoint. He analyses its structure, then muses over teachers' views of it as middle-class outdated fantasy. It fulfils the dreams of *all* freedom-loving children, he believes, and adds comfort because it is essentially 'snug'. Grahame's careful blend of human and animal is compared with the anthropomorphized rabbits in *Watership Down* and humans in animal disguise like Paddington.

Some Thoughts on Animals in Children's Books
MARY RAYNER *See page 42.*

Fantasy: Double Cream or Instant Whip? NEIL PHILIP
1981 M 82-90 An exploration of fantasy as the 'other' used to explore the familiar, not escape from it. 'Much fantasy writing ... offers only a simplistic daydream, not a literary experience.' Susan Cooper's work is examined in the light of the author's definition: only *The Dark Is Rising* passes the test.

Magical Thought in Story ANNE WILSON
1981 S 138-51 In an analysis of the differences between imaginative, rational thought and a process the author has isolated as 'magical thought', she draws a comparison between the battle of wits through which Jim Hawkins comes to understand the motivation of Israel Hands in *Treasure Island* (imaginative thought) and Jack's outwitting of the giant no less than three times in 'Jack and the Beanstalk' (magical thought). The hero of the folk tale is himself the teller of a tale that is his own free 'magical' thinking. 'The Golden Bird' is another example; and Daphne du Maurier's *Rebecca* is seen as an example of the unnamed heroine's 'magical thought' about adulthood.

Tom's Midnight Garden and the Vision of Eden NEIL PHILIP
1982 J 21-5 A discussion of two experiences of time, 'line' and 'loop', in Philippa Pearce's *Tom's Midnight Garden*; and a study of the vision of Eden and the loss of innocence in this modern classic and in the work of William Mayne and Helen Cresswell.

The Novels of Robert C. O'Brien BRIAN MORSE *See page 41.*

Joan Aiken JOHN ROWE TOWNSEND *See page 33.*

Rediscovering *The Little White Horse* JOHN GOUGH *See page 38.*

Tarzan the Incomparable TOVE JANSSON *See page 39.*

What Is Magic? ANNE WILSON
1988 S 170-80 A further exploration (see above) of magic—'a system of thought at a primitive level of the mind where all thinking and feeling have the power to bring things about (in the mind) ... the more helpless human beings feel the more they will use it.' From the medi-

eval romances to *Jane Eyre* and *Rebecca* there is 'magic' in stories. A comparison between 'The Goose Girl' (Grimm) and its 'magic' and L.M. Montgomery's *Anne of Green Gables*, which depends on human relationships for the same outcome, illuminates the thesis.

Lucy Boston, Storyteller PETER HOLLINDALE *See page 34.*

Poetry and Pirates: Swallows and Amazons at Sea
VICTOR WATSON *See page 68.*

Rupert in Space and Time HUGH CRAGO *See page 69.*

HISTORY OF CHILDREN'S BOOKS

This section includes pre-1918 authors and illustrators. The Signal Reprints series appears on pages 82-3. The annotations are arranged chronologically by publication date in *Signal*.

Pathetic Simplicity: An Introduction to Hesba Stretton and Her Books for Children LANCE SALWAY
1970 J 20-8 A survey, with special reference to *Jessica's First Prayer* (1867), in which, as in most of her work, a 'surface simplicity' conceals 'a serious philanthropic intention'.
1970 M 40-1 Jill E. Grey questions premise of article; Lance Salway responds.

Nursery Books of the Eighteenth Century
CHARLOTTE YONGE
1970 M 50-8 A nineteenth-century reviewer looks back at children's books of the eighteenth: at Barbauld, at Trimmer, at Wollstonecraft's adaptations of C.S. Salzman, at French fairy tales, at *The Looking Glass for the Mind* and at Rousseau. 'The age of sentiment and improbability was waning, and with the nineteenth century reason came into the nursery, and with it realism and purpose strong.'

Didactic Fiction CHARLOTTE YONGE
1970 S 103-11 A mid-nineteenth-century view of the didactic fiction

of the late eighteenth and early nineteenth centuries—a reaction against the excesses that sparked off the French Revolution. Maria Edgeworth, Mary Lamb, Hannah More, Mrs Sherwood, the Religious Tract Society come under the microscope as do information books ('walks with fathers, mothers, maiden aunts and governesses') and the effect of romance in stories on boys and on girls. Also discussed: traditional tales.

Class Literature of the Last Thirty Years CHARLOTTE YONGE
1971 J 35-43   In 1869 a critic classifies and criticizes the literature available to the young in mid-Victorian Britain: the moral story, the novel, literature for the poor, modern fairy stories (*The Water Babies*, 1863; *Alice's Adventures in Wonderland*, 1867), boys' books, girls' books, books about children, books for teachers, evangelism, and the narrowing effect of writing about each class for each class of reader referred to.

Remembering Richard Doyle ALAN MORLEY
1971 M 78-84   Richard Doyle deserves to rank with Caldecott, Crane, Cruikshank and Greenaway as a great nineteenth-century illustrator. His reputation as an illustrator for children rests on his work for John Ruskin's *King of the Golden River* (1851) and on *In Fairyland* (1870), for which Edmund Evans made the engravings.

The Basket of Flowers **by Christoph von Schmid** ANNE RENIER
1972 J S3-S22   A checklist of over 130 copies of *The Basket of Flowers* (1823; some translations carried the subtitle *Piety and Truth Triumphant*) held in the Renier Collection; prefaced by a brief account of its publishing history. Produced as an inserted supplement and available separately.

Letters to Two Children BEATRIX POTTER
1972 M 74-80   Two hitherto unpublished letters from Potter to children who had written to her.

The Cinderella Story 1724-1919 IRENE WHALLEY
1972 M 49-62   An examination of the versions of 'Cinderella' in the National Art Library at the Victoria and Albert Museum reveals changing attitudes to morals, to childhood and to the importance of illustration. The illustrators are considered as a reflection of publishers' changing view of their task. English translation of the French text is also examined.

The Emancipated Child in the Novels of E. Nesbit
MARY CROXSON
1974 M 51-64   The children in E. Nesbit's stories are freed from the Victorian conventions: by their dialogue, action and play they embody the hopes of the new century and the ideas of its progressive educational theorist, Froebel.

Castle Building FRANCES ELIZA CROMPTON
1978 S 138-43   Writing in the third person in 1894, Frances Eliza Crompton describes her childhood imaginings, her storytelling to her family, her writing, writing, writing and her dismay at 'betrayal' by her sister. Also discussed: plays, toy theatre.

Frances Eliza Crompton BARBARA BRILL
1979 M 88-102   The life of Frances Eliza Crompton as reflected in her numerous short stories and her many novels, often connected with the countryside, written between 1888 and 1903. Complete bibliography.

Using the Osborne Collection Facsimiles
GABRIELLE MAUNDER   *See page 51.*

Morals and Magic for Victorian Children ANNE WILSON
1982 M 88-102   A review of J.S. Bratton's *The Impact of Victorian Children's Fiction*, in the course of which Anne Wilson applies her own codification of stories into 'magical' and 'imaginative' (see 'Magical Thought in Story', page 74) to four of the Victorian children's novels covered by Bratton (von Schmid, Stretton, Wetherell, Ballantyne). Audiences look *at* a story, not *through* it, and therefore much symbolism in an imaginative story goes unnoticed.

History and Harvey Darton ALAN TUCKER
1982 M 113-28   A rave review, with extended entertaining asides, of F. J. Harvey Darton's *Children's Books in England* in its third edition (1982; Brian Alderson, editor). Darton is 'the Linnaeus of critics' since it was he who sorted, classified and listed the books, and 'established, one hopes for ever, that the children's book world is the creation and domain of the middle classes'. Tucker suggests that children's books 'are a microcosm of history, more, that children's reading is a major factor in the creation of a civilized society'.

[Sophie Cottin]. **Who Remembers** *Elizabeth?* M. NANCY CUTT
See page 127.

[J.M. Barrie]. **Fly Away, Peter?** NICHOLAS TUCKER *See page 97.*

Endpapers 1983 M 112-13 *Children's Literature Societies*
by Dennis Butts.

Another Side to Catherine Sinclair M. NANCY CUTT
1983 S 172-84   Sinclair's opposition to the 'unchristian quality of
stereotyped Evangelism' is examined in relation to her family life and
the times she lived in. By why did she not follow up the success of *Holi-day House* (1839) for over fifteen years?

The Tailors of Gloucester RICHARD HOUGH
1983 S 150-4   In comparing Beatrix Potter's original holograph of *The
Tailor of Gloucester* with the privately printed edition and with Warne's
first published edition—which reduced the 92 pages to 60—Richard
Hough feels readers have been deprived of a certain richness in the
longer version.

The Black Rabbit JOHN GOLDTHWAITE *See page 65.*

All of a Tremble to See His Danger AIDAN CHAMBERS
1986 S 193-212   A May Hill Arbuthnot Lecture. An analysis of Mark
Twain's *Huckleberry Finn*—as an American literary classic, as a novel that
speaks for adolescence to adolescent and adult, as an anti-slavery fiction
that has been misunderstood by those who don't respond to its irony.
Its didacticism is disputed, Twain's aim having been to enable readers to
think for themselves about slavery and freedom, children and parents.
The novel's humour, its use of demotic language and its relationship to
The Adventures of Tom Sawyer are also discussed.

Looking at Picture Books Again: *Sing a Song for Sixpence*
TESSA ROSE CHESTER *See page 90.*

Sis Beatrix JOHN GOLDTHWAITE
1987 M,S 117-37, 161-77   The Brer Rabbit stories of Joel Chandler
Harris had a profound influence on Beatrix Potter (as did, to a lesser
degree, Ewing, Dickens, Molesworth as writers, Caldecott and Lear as
artists). Her great achievement was the 'translation of folklore into the

kind of intimate book that is at once a mature world of emphatic art and unmistakably ... a book for young children'. A detailed analysis of *Mr Tod, The Flopsy Bunnies* and *Peter Rabbit*, tracing the similarities between these tales and Uncle Remus, forms the second part of this long essay.

A Sense of History GILLIAN AVERY
1988 J 53-72   A Woodfield Lecture. A survey of children's literature from the eighteenth century to the present day as a resource for social historians: ideology,   censorship, religion, fairy tales, research, and the author's own view of the material she read as a child. Comment also on the classics—mainly adult literature (*Robinson Crusoe, Gulliver's Travels*) or children's novels (Yonge, Ewing) that adults enjoy.

'Just really what they do', or, Re-reading Mrs Molesworth
JANE COOPER
1988 S 181-96   Mrs Molesworth's dialogue, her understanding of naughtiness, her philosophy of trust between parent and child, her use of crisis as a catalyst and her perception of the importance of food put her in the vanguard of realist writers for children. Her use of babytalk is discussed in relation to other Victorian writers.

Realism and Surrealism in Wonderland: John Tenniel and Anthony Browne   JANE DOONAN   *See page 85.*

Perspectives in Prose: Re-reading Some of Mrs Ewing's Stories   MARGERY FISHER
1989 M 118-26   Mrs Ewing's training in the visual arts enhanced her literary skill: her grasp of perspective, in particular, enabled her to draw the reader's attention 'to important points in a narrative by an unobtrusive but skilled use of distance'. The author commends Ewing's 'ability to suggest mental pictures through a scrupulous choice of actively pictorial words'. Attention is also drawn to the fine balance of Ewing's prose and Caldecott's illustrations. Also discussed: Philippa Pearce.

Sturdy Republicans: Nineteenth-Century American Children   GILLIAN AVERY
1989 S 195-210   American children's novels and magazines in the nineteenth century reflect the hard life of pioneer communities: they value home life, self-reliance, hard work, making money, resourcefulness, with the mother very much the formative influence. But there is a

distinction between pre-Civil War literature (when there was no time for childhood) and post-Civil War, when magazines such as *The Riverside, Saint Nicholas, Wide Awake* flourished. Comparisons are drawn with British publications of the period; similarities between Tarkington's *Penrod* and Crompton's 'William' books commented upon.

A Bear in the Nursery: Richard Hengist Horne
Writing for Children   MARGERY FISHER
1990 J 27-41 A pen picture of Horne and a tribute to his commitment when writing for children; his partnership with Mary Gillies under the pseudonym Harriet Myrtle; his creation of 'an individual narrator to whom he gave complete freedom of speech' in *Memoirs of a London Doll* (1846) by 'Mrs Fairstar'.

Brenda and Her Works   CHARLOTTE LENNOX-BOYD
1990 M 114-30 Brenda was less concerned to preach the church doctrine than to arouse the interest of the middle and upper classes in the plight of the poor. *Froggy's Little Brother* (1874) and her other books are clarion calls to duty rather than evangelist tracts.

Lost from the Nursery: Women Writing Poetry for
Children 1800 to 1850   MORAG STYLES
1990 S 177-205 The women poets of the early nineteenth century have disappeared from view, but they were important (not minor, as the Opies, and other anthologists, claim) in their innovations: subject matter, empathy, cradle songs, the voice of the child. The article is divided into three parts: in the first, four women poets (Jane and Ann Taylor, Adelaide O'Keefe and Elizabeth Turner) are highlighted; in the second, the author looks at hymns and social issues, such as the slave trade deplored in the poems of Lucy Aiken and Anna Barbauld; and in the third, she attends to the many poems written by women but uncredited—and to the status of Dorothy Wordsworth. Modern feminists tend to disregard women's poetry of the early nineteenth century because of its domestic assumptions.

'A welly serious thing': Carroll's *Sylvie and Bruno*   JOHN SPINK
1990 S 221-8 *Sylvie and Bruno* (1889) and *Sylvie and Bruno Concluded* (1893) belong to a small group of unreadable books by great writers. Lacking urgency, unity and cohesion, they are the work not of 'Lewis Carroll' but of Charles Dodgson, sadder, less fulfilled and ageing, who had 'lost the key to Wonderland'. Also discussed: Catherine Sinclair,

Holiday House, Harry Furniss, illustration.

Finnish Children's Literature RIITTA KUIVASMÄKI
See page 129.

Stories from a Victorian Nursery MARGERY FISHER
1992 S 176-89 Looking at children's books of the 1880s left to her by her mother-in-law, Margery Fisher compares them with current fiction for the middle years. She enjoys their 'energy, resourcefulness ... and candour', finds the language much richer (no 'staccato television-affected sentences'), the moral and religious didacticism replaced by modern concern for conservation, and wonders whether the 'confident use of the hierarchy of classes' is any less acceptable than 'the sometimes cringing self-consciousness about ethnic minorities, the finicking inverted snobbery in many descriptions of school classroom alliances', etc.

The Patrick Hardy Lecture JAN MARK
1994 J 19-36 The editor of *The Oxford Book of Children's Stories* surveys 250 years of stories for children, pointing out that the genre predated short stories for adults by two hundred years, and relates to the contemporary novel. She discusses the skill of short-story writing, the didacticism of the Victorian story, and the many social issues that are in evidence.
    1994 M 149-50 Neil Philip refutes Jan Mark's charge against John Buchan of anti-Semitism. JM replies.

Trying to Be Good ALAN TUCKER
1994 J 63-71 An extended review of Jan Mark's *The Oxford Book of Children's Stories*, 'the story of the story, told by itself', expresses doubts about the editor's application, in the Introduction, of the politics of 1994 to stories written at earlier periods, but commends her skill as an anthologist. 'At a time when Dorling Kindersley and encyclopaedias are dominating the children's market, and fiction reading has been Blytoned yet again by a handful of pop authors, perhaps [reading this book] would be another way to begin to open up the imagination: to see "the story" as a "fact" to be turned over in the mind, not a sofa to curl up in.'

These Piglets Fled Away PETER HOLLINDALE
1994 M 141-8 Hollindale highlights the diffidence with which other

critics suggest greatness for Beatrix Potter in the English literary or artistic tradition. She herself resisted such claims when they were made for her work by Janet Adam Smith and, in ironist fashion, by Graham Greene. Also discussed: *The Tale of Pigling Bland*, John Keats, 'The Eve of St Agnes'.

Madame de Ségur, Ideal Grandmother GWEN MARSH
See page 129.

Books for the First Enterers GILLIAN AVERY
1994 S 194-208 What did children read before books were produced specially for them in the mid nineteenth century? The author looks at fables and ballads, at school books and especially at the contribution of James Janeway, whose *Token for Children* (1671-2) was about children and for children a century ahead of Newbery. She also refers to seventeenth-century attitudes to the old romances, to learning to read in the past and to the influence of illustrators in making nursery rhymes into child lore.

Signal Reprints edited by LANCE SALWAY
This series was intended to indicate the immense variety of writing about children's books in the Victorian period and shortly after. Signal Reprints developed into Lance Salway's anthology, *A Peculiar Gift: Nineteenth Century Writings on Books for Children* (1977).

Introduction 1972 J 3.
All for Love, and No Reward: A.L.O.E. and Her
Books for Children EMMA MARSHALL (1897)
    1972 J 5-12 She wrote for 'God's blessing upon my attempts to instruct the lambs'.
Fairy Stories JOHN RUSKIN (1868)
    1972 M 81-6 Reaction against didacticism. Praise for Cruikshank's illustrations for Grimm.
Children's Fairy Tales and George Cruikshank
WILLIAM CALDWELL ROSCOE (1854)
    1972 S 115-22 The rewriting of fairy tales to serve political and social purposes deplored. Cruikshank's cuts admired.
Jules Verne at Home MARIE BELLOC LOWNDES (1895)
    1973 J 3-13 Interview reveals Verne's admiration for English adventure stories and explores absence of women in his own.

Should Children Have a Special Literature?
EDWARD SALMON (1890)
   1973 M 94-101   Yes. Excellence of Stevenson, Reed, Alcott, Molesworth; but parents lack knowledge and prices must be cheap.
Notes on My Own Books for Children
WALTER CRANE (1913)
   1974 J 10-15   Crane's apprenticeship, work with Evans, new technology and an assessment of children's view of art in books.
Mrs Barbauld CATHERINE J. HAMILTON (1892)
   1974 M 70-84   Her life; the school book (*Early Lessons*; *Hymns in Prose*) of the eighteenth century.
Personal Reminiscences R.M. BALLANTYNE (1893)
   1974 S 141-53   Research for the historical adventure story; publishing in the nineteenth century.
The Fantastic Imagination GEORGE MacDONALD (1908)
   1975 J 26-32   Refusal to define fairy tale or fantasy: depth and music of the words, not the meaning, are important.
The Parent's Assistant AUSTIN DOBSON (1911)
   1975 M 96-104   A researcher's problems in tracing editions of Maria Edgeworth's moral tales for the Georgian nursery.
The Reading of the Modern Girl FLORENCE B. LOW (1906)
   1975 S 118-30   The importance of literature (as life); poor teaching methods in schools; and the lowering of standards through magazines and public libraries.
Recollections of Lewis Carroll HARRY FURNISS (1908)
   1976 J 45-50   The illustrator's problems when working with Carroll.
Bad Literature for the Young ALEXANDER STRAHAN (1875)
   1976 M 83-95   Should the penny dreadful be censored to protect the poor (should they be taught to read?) and others? More pernicious than fairy tales. Also discussed: magazines.
Fairy Tales as Literature UNA ASHWORTH TAYLOR (1898)
   1976 S 123-38; 1977 J 48-56. The fairy tale in Italy, France and (Part 2) Germany is part of the literature and social history of each.

ILLUSTRATORS & ILLUSTRATING, PICTURE BOOKS & COMIC STRIPS

The annotations on pages 84-8 are arranged alphabetically by the illustrator concerned; the general articles, pages 88-90, are arranged chronologically by publication date in *Signal*.

A Certain Particularity: An Interview with Janet and Allan Ahlberg ELAINE MOSS

1990 J 20-6   The Ahlbergs' interweaving of talents produced high quality picture books that also achieved huge sales worldwide. The traditional tale, humour, the balance of word and image, production and editorial problems as well as Allan's poetry and Janet's obsession with wartime working-class Britain discussed.

Celebrating Edward Ardizzone on his Seventieth Birthday 16th October 1970

1970 S 67-72   Reproductions of the artist's selection of some favourite illustrations drawn by him for children.

The Born Illustrator EDWARD ARDIZZONE

1970 S 73-80   The born illustrator came to the fore with the rise of the novel; his creative imagination is freed by the written word, he draws from his mind rather than from life and at his best he adds a third dimension to the books. Ardizzone compares Keene and Cruikshank, talks of the revival of book design in the 1920s and 1930s which gave work to painters and poster artists rather than the professional illustrator. Modern (1958) teaching methods and tricks of the trade are also included.

Edward Ardizzone GABRIEL WHITE

1980 J 8-10   At the launch party for his *Edward Ardizzone*—one week after Ardizzone's death—Gabriel White recalled some happy memories.

Pauline Baynes: Mistress of the Margin ELAINE MOSS

1973 M 88-93   In an interview Pauline Baynes talks about her early life and wartime service, her passion for the mediaeval period (*A Dictionary of Chivalry*), her botanical and zoological paintings for Helen Piers's *The Snail and the Caterpillar*, and she describes her association with J.R.R. Tolkien over *The Lord of the Rings* and C.S. Lewis over the Narnia series.

Quentin Blake ELAINE MOSS
1975 J 33-9 In an interview Quentin Blake talks about his early career, working for *Punch*, his entry into children's books through John Ryder. He describes his own books as 'pictures with words added', talks about the challenges of illustrating Russell Hoban's *How Tom Beat Captain Najork and his Hired Sportsmen* and discusses illustrating novels and Michael Rosen's poetry as well as the influence of film.

Raymond Briggs: On British attitudes to the strip cartoon and children's book illustration ELAINE MOSS
1979 J 26-33 Raymond Briggs speaks of his art-school training, work in advertising and the 897 pictures for the *Mother Goose Treasury* as preparation for his cartoon picture books—*The Snowman, Father Christmas*, etc., for the young and *Fungus the Bogeyman* for adolescent readers. He speaks with passion about the appreciation of strip cartoon as an art form in Europe, of the placing of the speech bubble in the frame as a psychological message. Also discussed: Greenaway Medal.

Talking Pictures: A New Look at *Hansel and Gretel*
JANE DOONAN
1983 S 123-31 A detailed, page-by-page analysis of the art and symbolism in Anthony Browne's *Hansel and Gretel*. Browne penetrates the tale itself whereas most current illustration of folk and fairy tale is either trivial and oversweet, or so beautiful that the text is overpowered, or an embellishment that adds nothing.

Realism and Surrealism in Wonderland: John Tenniel and Anthony Browne JANE DOONAN
1989 J 9-30 *Alice's Adventures in Wonderland* as interpreted by two illustrators over a century apart. Sir John Tenniel, the first illustrator (1865) of *Alice* (after Carroll's own attempt), worked in the golden age of book illustration (Burne-Jones, Hughes, Holman Hunt); he conveyed the matter-of-fact actuality of the unreality as effectively as the text with which his illustrations were integrated (by the Dalziell Brothers' wood-engraving technique). Anthony Browne (1988) uses brightly coloured, highly focused twentieth-century surrealist devices as the visual language for the depiction of Alice's unconscious. Both sets of illustrations are discussed in detail, including the anthropomorphism.

Notes on My Own Books for Children WALTER CRANE
See page 83.

Children's Fairy Tales and George Cruikshank
WILLIAM CALDWELL ROSCOE *See page 82.*

Remembering Richard Doyle ALAN MORLEY *See page 76.*

Recollections of Lewis Carroll HARRY FURNISS *See page 83.*

Kathleen Hale and Orlando the Marmalade Cat ELAINE MOSS
1972 S 123-7   In an interview Kathleen Hale speaks of her childhood
and 'near delinquency', her bohemian life and the extraordinary publishing history of the first Orlando book 'in seven colours, a totally
uneconomic proposition'. The Orlando books had texts that were
written to appeal to parents ('Why make reading to children ... a
bore?') but the storyline, the characters and the pictures of Orlando and
his family were for children, especially the evacuees of World War II.

'Where's Tha Colours?': Shirley Hughes at Work
ELAINE MOSS
1980 M 74-80   In an interview that touches on children's need for a
'good nourishing mix' of all kinds of illustration at all ages as well as on
illiteracy and graphics, Shirley Hughes concentrates on narrative illustration in picture books and describes in detail the challenges she faced
in producing the wordless strip cartoon *Up and Up.*

Pat Hutchins: A Natural ELAINE MOSS
1973 J 32-6   In an interview Pat Hutchins talks of her early life as the
one-but-youngest of a large family (*Titch*), of the wordless picture book
Changes, Changes, of colour separation for all her books until she was
allowed full colour for *Good-night, Owl!*, of being published first in the
US and therefore being ineligible at that time for either the Caldecott
or the Greenaway Medals. Also discussed: *Rosie's Walk*, Susan
Hirschman.

The Idle Bear and the Active Reader JANE DOONAN
1988 J 33-47   A philosophical visual analysis of an outwardly simple-
looking teddy-bear picture book by Robert Ingpen: 'the scale of the
temporal dimensions in *The Idle Bear* is the source of its richness' so the
author considers four aspects of time in relation to it: the artist's time in
creating the book; physical and aesthetic time taken by the reader to
absorb the experience; the time before the story opens, since the bears
in it are old; the time after the story ends, since the bears will survive

the 'interlude' that is the book. Annotated reference list appended, including the work of Nelson Goodman, Ciaran Benson, Susanne Langer.

Two Artists Telling Tales: Chihiro Iwasaki and Lisbeth Zwerger JANE DOONAN
1984 M 93-102 An analysis of the techniques used by a Japanese artist, Chihiro Iwasaki, and an Austrian, Lisbeth Zwerger, in illustrating picture-book versions of traditional tales. Both are concerned with the emotion of the story, neither supplies superfluous detail. Iwasaki 'tells us more about herself than about Andersen' in her *The Red Shoes*; Zwerger 'offers a lightly personal interpretation of a story from the European tradition, Grimms' *Little Red Cap*'.

Josef Lada, Illustrator STUART AMOR *See page 125.*

Chiyoko Nakatani ELAINE MOSS
1973 S 135-8 After discussing the influence of Japanese art on French Impressionists (and French Impressionists on the Japanese) Nakatani declares herself the child of two Europeans, Bettina Hürlimann (who sent her Alberti's *The Animals' Lullaby* to illustrate) and Paul Faucher (Père Castor), who asked for a Japanese sea story with high quality Japanese paintings: he got *Fumio and the Dolphins*.

Introduction from *The Drawings of Mervyn Peake*
MERVYN PEAKE
1970 J 16-19 'Art is the ultimate sorcery', says Peake, arguing that pictures change as the eye of the beholder gains in experience of looking.

Tony Ross: Art to Enchant JANE DOONAN
1985 J 34-43 An examination of line, colour and page design in the work of Tony Ross, including an analysis of his *Puss in Boots*. Doonan is concerned that picture-book artists who are unaware of the deeper significance of a fairy tale may, by their pictorial interpretation of it, diminish what it offers.

Richard Scarry ELAINE MOSS
1974 J 42-6 In an interview the prolific artist expounds his aims: respect for children coupled with instruction and plenty of fun (*What Do People Do All Day?*); expansion of vocabulary (*Best Word Book Ever*); the use of animal characters instead of people for easy identification (and

avoidance of the race issue); the glory of being sold in supermarkets; and his indifference to librarians and the Caldecott Medal.

Outside Over There: A Journey in Style   JANE DOONAN
1986 M,S 92-103,172-87   In a two-part article the author considers in detail Maurice Sendak's *Outside Over There* first as a visual work of art which has its iconographic roots in the Northern Romantic tradition of Runge, William Blake, Friedrich in particular. Its quasi-religious nature is observed, as is the change of mode within one picture book. In the second part of the article the author discusses Sendak's use of multiple perspective, inviting the reader to float, the way tension is created by the twin forces of direction and weight and his extraordinary mastery of sequence in the picture book. In *Where the Wild Things Are*, *In the Night Kitchen* and *Outside Over There* Sendak gives precise delineation to the fantasies of childhood. References to work of Rudolf Arnheim, E.H. Gombrich, Frederick Gore, Robert Rosenblum.

An Interview with Maurice Sendak   CHARLOTTE F. OTTEN
1992 M 110-27   In an interview Sendak talks extensively about his illustrations for Randall Jarrell's *Fly by Night* ('it's that excruciating sense of hanging in space ... but also the incredible sensuality'). He also talks of illustrating Grimm for *The Juniper Tree* and how the fathers in these stories foreshadowed the father 'at sea' in Sendak's own creation, the picture book *Outside Over There*.

Into the Dangerous World: *We Are All in the Dumps with Jack and Guy* by Maurice Sendak   JANE DOONAN
1994 S 155-71   A retrospective look at Maurice Sendak's picture books culminating in a detailed analysis of the inspiration for and the techniques used in ...*Jack and Guy*. The author also considers the older audience now created for picture books; and she discusses Sendak's concern to highlight the extreme poverty of the US urban underclass. Also discussed: Andrea Mantegna, *Descent into Limbo*, Christian iconography.

Cushla and Her Books DOROTHY BUTLER *See page 48.*

'Them's for the Infants, Miss': Some Misguided Attitudes to Picture Books for the Older Reader ELAINE MOSS

1978 M,S 66-72,144-9 John Burningham's *Come Away from the Water, Shirley* spearheads a primary school librarian's determined attack on prejudice against using picture books with older children. Anno, Michael Foreman, Hoban and Blake, Graham Oakley and Raymond Briggs—because of their social and political satire—become sought after both by ten-year-olds reading E. Nesbit and by those still struggling with Dr Seuss. In the second article the positive use of comic strips (*Asterix* and *Tintin*) is described, the work of Charles Keeping, champion of the world of the underprivileged urban child, is highlighted and the multiculturalism and role reversal in *Mother Goose Comes to Cable Street* commented upon.

1982 S 197-9 Elaine Moss recommends new titles for *Picture Books for Young People 9-13*, her Signal Bookguide.

1983 J 53 Letter from librarians Catherine Blanshard and Janet Hill about *Picture Books . . . 9-13*.

1983 M 113-16 **Endpapers** *Picture Books & Older Readers* by Catherine Blanshard and Janet Hill.

W(h)ither Picture Books? Some Tricks of the Trade
ELAINE MOSS

1980 J 3-7 In a recessionary market dominated by the sale of international rights the traditional picture book with a text and a story is being sidelined by gimmickry: pop-ups, books as puzzle/treasure hunt (Kit Williams's *Masquerade*), books of paintings (Helen Bradley's *And Miss Carter Wore Pink*), split-page books (Graham Oakley's up-market *Magical Changes*, an exception that highlights the slide towards books of board games), etc.

1980 M 115-16 Nicola Bennetts disagrees about *Masquerade*.

Picture Books There and Here ELAINE MOSS
1983 M 72-6 A consideration of Barbara Bader's *American Picture Books from Noah's Ark to the Beast Within* sparks off a comparison of American picture books with British, the influence of the pre-1914 British artists (Crane, Caldecott, Potter, etc.) on American picture books, the cultural isolation of Britain from Europe in a period of immigration which brought many central European families to the New World.

Taking a Good Look at Picture Books CELIA BERRIDGE
See page 62.

Who Does Snow-White Look At? HUGH CRAGO
1984 S 129-145   Four picture-book versions of Snow-White (two 'mass-market', two 'quality') looked at from the point of view of messages a child would receive about the story from *only* the pictures in each. Aspects include: the covers and preliminary openings; Nature; Snow-White and the Queen; the Dwarfs and Men versus feeling and acting. The Japanese board book and the Disney version share with Nancy Ekholm Burkert's in the criticism as being too positive: they 'act' rather than feel. Trina Schart Hyman's illustrations convey the emotional messages of the fairy tale.

Looking at Picture Books Again: *Sing a Song for Sixpence*
TESSA ROSE CHESTER
1987 J 32-7   Caldecott as the 'pivotal figure' within the tradition of narrative illustration that is peculiarly English. The ideas in Brian Alderson's *Sing a Sing for Sixpence* are not original but his application of them directly to the picture book 'exploring the links between the different exponents of the narrative tradition in meticulous detail' is warmly welcomed.

Invisible Pictures PHILIP PULLMAN   *See page 67.*

The Constructedness of Texts: Picture Books and the Metafictive DAVID LEWIS   *See page 67.*

Drawing Winners: The Kate Greenaway Nominations 1991
JANE DOONAN
1992 S 202-14   Jane Doonan looks at the six nominations for the Kate Greenaway Medal (illustrations by Ahlberg, Oxenbury, French, Binch, Lynch, J. Baker and Ray), selecting two for detailed study. Jeannie Baker's *Window* is an irony—a picture book about all kinds of blindness (to conservation issues): its method, viewpoint, central figure as concept, time factors and the natural materials for the collage echoing its green theme are commented upon. Jane Ray's *The Story of Christmas* ('a pictorial equivalence for Christmas carolling') is compared with religious art of the Renaissance, its symbolism, iconography and freshness.

A Puffin Illustrator of the Forties SHEILA JACKSON
See page 109.

INFORMATION BOOKS

The annotations are arranged chronologically by publication date in *Signal*.

Information Books: A few home thoughts about the T.E.S. Awards and about television's effects on publishing
ELAINE MOSS
1978 J 25-9 *Man and Machines*, one of the ten volumes in Mitchell Beazley's Joy of Knowledge Encyclopaedia, receives the Senior *Times Educational Supplement* Information Book Award. Its doublespread-per-topic approach, multi-authorship, team of visualizers, make it a close relation of television, whereas Richard Mabey's *Street Flowers*, the Junior Award recipient, is a book by a single, enthusiastic communicator.

Choosing Information Books JENNIFER WILSON
1982 S 163-8 'Cut-and-dried packages of knowledge which they are asked to swallow'—often by unnamed authors—will not stimulate children's dialogue with a text, which is essential to exploration of a subject. A plea for both narrative and the authorial voice in information books and for a more frequent question: 'How do we know?'

Creation to Civilization HUGH CRAGO
1983 M 97-107 Remembering how he learned about the world as a child—through good storytellers like Hendrik Van Loon—the author looks at information books (and other media such as television) and regrets both the absence of story and the way spectacular events have stolen the limelight at the expense of a framework based on time. He notes the 'vocabulary of imperialism' and power (e.g. amphibians 'colonizing' or 'invading'), the selective nature of social history (tools rather than domestic developments) and the celebration of size and strength. A plea for 'androgynous' storytelling in the recounting of a history of civilization: Goodall's *Story of an English Village* is exemplary.

Information Books 1983: Weeds or Flowers?
JENNIFER WILSON

1984 M 112-19   A critic and selector of information books discloses the questions she asks of the contenders before her, believing that the few flowers in the field could, without energetic weeding of the submissions, be choked. She sees danger in the information book for schools becoming the equivalent of the reading scheme in fiction, believes the doublespread presentation to be a straitjacket. Writing should be accessible, enthusiastic and open-ended—continuing an ongoing conversation, providing a better focus, then leaving it with growing points for further exploration.

The Last Days in the Old Home   HUGH CRAGO

1989 J 51-70   Arthur Mee's Children's Encyclopaedia with its mix of fact and fiction retains its place in the affection of the author, who is nevertheless severe in his criticism. The vocabulary is one of capitalist imperialism combined with the Romantic ideals of heroism, loyalty, honour—'our side' always being the victor. It is therefore myth as much as knowledge, all couched in language that is confident, aggressive and masculine. The gulf between it and the culture of the late twentieth century is unbridgeable.

LEARNING TO READ

The annotations are arranged chronologically by publication date in *Signal*.

Learning to Read: An Essay with some Victorian examples of Reading Games   ALAN TUCKER

1977 S 122-39   A historical survey of methods of teaching reading from Victorian times through i.t.a. to speed reading (with photographic examples of reading games). Alan Tucker believes that the restriction of language and ideolect in a visual age results in a reduced spoken vocabulary which, since speech comes first, hinders progress in reading. Learning to read is equated with pathfinding (as in Konrad Lorenz's experiments) in animals. In the middle years an over-emphasis on spelling and 'correct' English can shut a child off from literature (a 'total landscape' of which should be offered in school) for life.

Accepting the Eleanor Farjeon Award DOROTHY BUTLER
1980 S 147-50   Dorothy Butler describes her Book Theatre in the
Auckland bookshop she owns and how by providing positive 'encouragement, experience, enrichment' her programme can counteract the
bossing, blaming, coaching and despair some children have been subjected to in trying to learn to read. She also describes the ethos of her
bookshop and her debt to Eleanor Farjeon.

Endpapers 1981 M 129-30 Jill Bennett updates her Signal Bookguide,
Learning to Read with Picture Books.

Books for the Under-Twos VALERIE WILLSHER
1982 M 103-12   While commenting on the characteristics most necessary in books for the under-twos (strong outline, relevant pictures) and
listing her own child's favourites, the author complains that libraries do
not offer to parents a showcase of suitable material. Also discussed:
board books.
   1982 S 196-7   Response from Gill Clayton, librarian, and Valerie
Willsher's reply.
   1983 J 53-4   Response from Ted Percy, librarian.

Thoughts on Margaret Meek's *Learning to Read*
VALERIE WILLSHER
1982 S 183-90   A librarian who is also the parent of a two-year-old
explores Margaret Meek's *Learning to Read*, in which she makes 'her
considerable experience and enthusiasm available to us'. The extended
review considers the first two years, the alphabet, parental expectations
of the child, books in school, the librarian's role.
   1983 M 116-18   *More thoughts on learning to read* by Mary O'Neill.

Help a Child to Read: An Interview with Susan Belgrave
ELAINE MOSS
1983 S 132-6   In celebration of the tenth anniversary of the Volunteer
Reading Help Scheme, Susan Belgrave describes her reasons for initi-
ating it (illiterate youngsters entering secondary education; truancy),
the bureaucratic problems in getting started, the selection and training
of volunteers and the mutual rewards (for children and helpers) that
result.

Books for the Special Child RACHEL ANDERSON
1985 M 120-5 A book-experienced parent reassesses her family's picture books in order to meet the needs of an adopted nine-year-old mentally handicapped son. She notes his pleasure, for instance, in the stable family pattern offered by most of the Ladybird Keyword Readers.

Texts and Training: Some Notes on the Metaphor of Reading as a Military Operation GEOFF WILLIAMS
1985 S 182-8 A tongue-in-cheek view of learning to read as it might be perceived through military metaphors (attack, strategy, equipment, armour) used in Teachers' Resource Books. How about using language itself as part of meaningful stories instead of the reading schemes? The casualties of war (so-called dyslexics) need *more* meaningful language, not less.

Read with Me **and After** LIZ WATERLAND
1986 S 147-55 'All children want to be readers and writers. It is the school that destroys their desire' affirms Liz Waterland, looking back on a year's further 'apprenticeship' after the publication of her *Read with Me*. Books, time and trust are identified as the three necessary elements in learning to become a reader—the book leading the teacher as well as the child in the process. In this retrospective Liz Waterland answers many of the questions the publication of her work has prompted, including 'What's wrong with reading schemes?'

Learning to Read with Picture Books: **An Anniversary**
JILL BENNETT
1989 S 156-9 The author of *Learning to Read with Picture Books* looks back on developments in the ten years since its publication. While welcoming the spread of its philosophy (and fearing that where misapplied it could itself become a kind of scheme) she deplores the split between those who favour 'real books' and those who champion 'reading schemes'.

Finding Their Levels While Losing Our Balance?
LIZ WATERLAND
1992 J 3-11 Using an album/diary format, the head of an infants' school, who has had success using picture books to help create readers, looks at the National Curriculum Standard Assessment Tests and, while questioning their validity and the thinking behind them, concludes

that 'we are lucky that much of what is asked can be bent to our own will'. She deplores the reductionist use of valuable material.

Transitions: The Notion of Change in Writing for Children MARGARET MEEK

1992 J 13-33   A Patrick Hardy Lecture. The National Curriculum's assumptions about uniformity in teaching methods, texts for practice, children's rate of development, and the ignorance of politicians about how reading, a reflective and recursive process, develops in *individuals*, all these raise the spectre of children's books being coded and graded into one giant reading scheme; the growth of understanding (over the last thirty years among educationists) about how and why children read is our bulwark against this. We now need a reflective understanding of the task of teaching reading and of reading itself; critics lack this approach, falling back on a 'final' vocabulary ('attractively illustrated' etc.). Also discussed: information books and visual literacy, children's storying, the wholeness of texts and how they change with rereading.

LIBRARIANSHIP

The annotations are arranged chronologically by publication date in *Signal*.

Accepting the Eleanor Farjeon Award JANET HILL

1972 S 109-14   Receiving the award for her *Books for Children: The Homelands of Immigrants in Britain*, edited in association with the Institute of Race Relations, Janet Hill spoke of the librarian who knows books and children being in a prime position to review, of the need to justify criticism and of Lambeth libraries' commitment to taking books out to the community.

At the Beginning EILEEN COLWELL

1974 J 30-7   The pioneer British children's librarian recalls her early days in the profession, her first children's library, the interest it aroused, her international contacts and the author visits she organized. She talks of buying books from Bumpus (see 'The Bumpus Years' by Eleanor Graham, page 45), of the founding of *The Junior Bookshelf* in 1936 and of only one children's librarian 'amongst a bevy of chief librarians' being on the selection committee for the newly instituted Carnegie Medal in 1937.

Eileen Colwell MARCUS CROUCH
1974 J 38-41   A seventieth-birthday tribute to Eileen Colwell, 'brilliant librarian, wise administrator, inspired educationalist—and storyteller extraordinary'. Changes in the status and direction of children's librarianship in the 1960s and 1970s are referred to.

A Visit to Japan EILEEN COLWELL
1986 M 109-17   As a pioneer children's librarian, Eileen Colwell reports mainly on the library provision for children in Japan in which the Bunko, the home library, takes precedence over the public library service. She describes lecturing (with an interpreter), storytelling, visits to publishers, bookshops (73 specializing in children's books), Japanese comics and Japanese children's television which varies 'from the silly to the horrific'. Translations of English books into Japanese far outnumber traffic in the other direction.

Librarians for Children Today PEGGY HEEKS
1992 J 34-40   Children have an entitlement to quality—yet in the 1970s and 1980s emphasis on management in the library service has led to a lack of specialization in children's work, book selection has set its sights on social concerns at the expense of literary quality and Local Management of Schools has threatened the Schools Library Service. In the 1990s the pursuit of quality and more precise targeting of resources may redeem the service.

OTHER MEDIA

After the Gate WILLIAM CORLETT
1980 M 107-13   A comparison between writing a teenage novel (*Gate of Eden*) and adapting it for television. Does a larger audience automatically give the author greater pleasure? Corlett says the bigger triumph is to 'reach one person (really reach so that he or she wears my skin and sees through my eyes) through the silent medium of reading a book'.

The Hunt for Evil ROBERT WESTALL

1981 J 3-13 A comparison between what young people read and what they see on television. In TV series such as *Starsky and Hutch* there is no good in the baddies, no bad in the goodies: death and destruction are (pornographically) portrayed without emotion. The same is true of Tolkien's *Lord of the Rings*: Jung accepted 'shadow' as part of ourselves but Tolkien abjures this and shows an emotionless slaughter of 'evil' by 'good'. On the screen our hate and fear are being pandered to by third-rate hacks.

1981 M 126-39 Neil Philip responds to *Lord of the Rings* comment; RW replies; telling points made about *Wizard of Earthsea* and C.S. Lewis's *Last Battle*.

Fly Away, Peter? NICHOLAS TUCKER

1982 J 43-9 An analysis of the enduring popularity of J.M. Barrie's *Peter Pan*, 'a play that gets so close to children's own fantasy life that it even includes various common violent, morbid or sadistic feelings normally omitted in child-centred writing'. Barrie's absorption in children's play gave him the deep understanding of childhood fears and fantasy life which bore fruit in *Peter Pan*.

1982 M 129-32 Corrective response from Neil Philip.

Peter Pan, Captain Hook and the Book of the Video
PETER HOLLINDALE

1993 S 152-75 Text and intertext in *Peter Pan* the play, *Peter Pan* the story (various versions authorized by Barrie for children of different ages and for adults), the Disney cartoon film, *Hook* (the Spielberg feature film) and the books spawned by the video; 'no classic text remains entirely static ... and there are particular reasons why the *Peter Pan* story is a protean, unstable and evolving one.'

POETRY

The annotations are arranged chronologically by publication date in *Signal*; the Signal Poetry Award is dealt with on pages 102-4. A list of poems published in *Signal* appears on page 105.

On Poetry and Children ALAN TUCKER
1970 J 7-15   Alan Tucker looks at the books of poetry published for the young in the preceding year (1969) and uses what he finds there as a springboard for his views on the vital importance of poetry in life. He argues that since religion is in decline and pure philosophy beyond the range of most of us, it is literature that brings us into contact with great minds (because it is explicit in a way painting and music cannot be). Therefore 'finished excellence' in what is offered to the young is essential.

 1970 M 36-40   Letters from Margaret Clark, challenging Alan Tucker's views, and Hugh Lyon, who disagrees with AT's verdict on Walter de la Mare. AT replies.

Dark Rainbow: Reflections on Ted Hughes JOHN ADAMS
1971 M 65-71   The publication of *Crow* prompts a critic to assess Ted Hughes's influence, as poet and selector of poetry, on children and teachers over the preceding decade. Hughes's admiration for the 'unimpeded efficiency and directness of the predatory instincts' in Nature (which some call violence), and his watchful stance, which precludes sympathetic involvement even with human beings, mean that children's excitement in reading Hughes will not develop into lifetime love of him as a poet. As an anthologist Hughes's desire to free children from what he calls 'the maternal octopus of ancient English poetic tradition' cuts them off from their own literary heritage.

Poetry, Children and Ted Hughes BRIAN MORSE
1971 S 102-13   In a refutation of John Adams's views on Ted Hughes (above) Brian Morse states his belief that Hughes, being contemporary and a man who is not running away from his deepest emotions, is a poet whose vividness can take its place beside the headlines. He examines in particular Hughes's *Wodwo* and *Crow*, in which man succeeds the animals as focal point. Morse believes 'trash art' is 'more corrupting to the imaginative life than violence intelligently placed and articulated'.

 1972 J 31-3   John Adams's letter of objection.

Skip-rope Rhymes: Some International Variations
FRANCELIA BUTLER
1973 J 19-31   Death, love, bawdy, exoticism, religion, food—these are the elements of skip-rope rhymes in the US and England, in Africa, the Soviet Union, Portugal and South East Asia. An examination, with examples of an active oral tradition.

The Oxford Book of Children's Verse edited by Iona &
Peter Opie   reviewed by ALAN TUCKER
1973 M 59-64   The reviewer sets *The Oxford Book of Children's Verse* in its context as part of the Oxford poetry anthology canon. He notes that the voice of innocence in poetry (Wordsworth, Blake) is replaced by 'knowingness' (Stevenson, de la Mare, Farjeon); also that verses reflecting 'politically incorrect' views have been consigned to Notes.

A Poetry-Book Survey ALAN TUCKER
1973 S 139-55   A poet looks at over two dozen anthologies, books in series or the work of individual poets published for the young in 1971-72 and in the course of reviewing them is prepared to define his expectation of poetry ('concentrated expression') and offer a methodological prescription for selecting poetry for children. He believes tradition must precede experiment, deplores the 'feedback of naivety', ponders on the value of Black verse that is negative, looks favourably only on the best in humorous verse and, in an epigrammatic conclusion, states 'Children lose themselves in novels. The idea is that they find themselves in poetry.'

The Key of the Kingdom GRISELDA GREAVES
1979 S 159-68   An anthologist extrapolates from her own lifelong experience of poetry its importance in the life of others. 'I do believe poetry to be essential to the human soul, and that a life without access to poetry is a life diminished.' The article is illuminated by poems of special significance to herself, to her children and to her pupils.

Living with Poetry MYFANWY THOMAS
1981 S 159-74   The daughter of Edward Thomas recalls life in the Thomas household and her own path towards 'trepidantly' becoming a teacher who could convey her own love of poetry to children of all ages and from all backgrounds.

Magic in the Poetry of Charles Causley NEIL PHILIP

1982 S 139-51   An overall view of Charles Causley's poetry, his narrative verse, his three-act musical play *Aucassin and Nicolette*, but principally the mystery and magic of his often Christian poetry. 'It is very rare to find poets who can hold steadily to their true magic, speak confidently in their own language and yet remain accessible to children.'

The Difficult Poem JOHN DANBY

1983 J 18-25   A reprinted chapter from John Danby's *Approach to Poetry* (1940) proposes that we should give children in school poetry that will grow as they grow, not the ephemeral: 'the thing is not how much experience we have but how much new experience we are capable of having'.

Nonsense and the Language of Poetry SUSAN T. VIGUERS

1983 S 137-49   An imaginary conversation between the author and Edward Lear's cat, Foss, on the inter-relationship of nonsense and successful verse. 'Nonsense opens the door to poetic truth,' says the author while Foss remarks (of Carroll's *Jabberwocky*) that he has created 'the weight of meaning without meaning'; the conclusion is that nonsense 'is immensely valuable as a form in itself, but it is also a key to the creations of the imagination and to creative understanding'.

An Interview with Norman Nicholson

PHILLIP HAY & ANGHARAD WYNN-JONES

1984 J 19-32   Two children (aged eleven and thirteen) interview the poet, who responds to their questions on the difference between prose and poetry; on his own early experience of traditional poetry; of the difference between good and bad poetry; the significance of place in poetry; the difference between poetry for children and for adults. He speaks of radio and TV and the danger of 'popularizing' the wrong sort of poetry, of the process of revision, and of young people writing free verse when they 'don't have anything to be free from'.

Inside the Lurking-Glass with Ted Hughes LISSA PAUL

1986 J 52-63   Taking up points made in earlier issues of *Signal* (Stephen Corrin, Mary Hillier, Alan Tucker, Neil Philip) Lissa Paul contends of Hughes's poetry that 'suitability for children' is not an issue: what matters is the poetry itself. Children, being more responsive (and less defensive) than adults, can be reached by a poet of Ted Hughes's calibre because he addresses the child-adult, allowing adults to listen secretly.

Referring to Neil Postman's *The Disappearance of Childhood* ('the horror and the joy of the world comes through the amoral lingua franca of television which contains no human value or response') she maintains 'that Hughes's poetry is redemptive, the language of our common humanity'.

Poetry by Heart JUNE BENN
1988 J 48-52 Learning poetry by heart in childhood—even minor verse—can lead to lifelong pleasure in poetry; an older reader looks back gratefully to the poetry books and poetry lessons at her Elementary School in the 1930s.
1988 M 150 Gordon Dennis supports these sentiments.

Taking Time ALAN TUCKER
1989 M 98-117 In celebration of the tenth anniversary of the Signal Poetry Award Alan Tucker was asked to look forward. But the future has a past. He provides a philosophy of poetry, traditional and modern, with special concern for the validity of the young experience (often under-rated). He hopes for 'if not a high style at least not quite such a low style in children's poetry', for a stronger critical sense (that does not, for example, condemn Milligan—who has written brilliantly against war—because of a racist remark), for more women and ethnic poets and for poetry in the future that grows from the work of Charles Causley and Ted Hughes. 'We can offer children what they may be persuaded to like.'

Lost from the Nursery: Women Writing Poetry for Children 1800 to 1850 MORAG STYLES See page 80.

On Receiving the Signal Poetry Award GERARD BENSON
1991 S 147-53 The poet recalls the stages of preparation for his award-winning anthology, *This Poem Doesn't Rhyme*.

Journey into Poetry ANNE HARVEY
1992 S 190-201 An autobiographical essay by the noted poetry anthologist.

Adlestrop and After JAN MARK
1993 M 94-102 Jan Mark describes her 'furtive pleasure' at primary school in *The Penguin Book of Comic and Curious Verse* and compares its contents with 'more bleeding fairies' (Allingham etc.)—until a new

teacher walked into the classroom and mesmerized even the boys with Rupert Brooke's 'Grantchester'. 'He simply stood before us and without fear offered us the thing he cared for most . . . We learned.' She also learned that understanding only comes with developing maturity and with this 'secret armour' managed to endure poetry lessons in her secondary school.

Questions of Poetry   JOHN MOLE
1994 M 86-92   The poet responds to questions that arose during the deliberations of the Signal Poetry Award selectors, beginning with 'What is poetry?'

The Signal Poetry Award
Major articles on the award winner and other poetry books published in the given year. Perennial concerns: what *real* poetry is; the pre-eminence of the single-poet collection; what makes a good anthology; the physical aspects—layout, illustration, typography—of poetry publication; the feebleness of most poetry written for children; subject matter, language; children writing poetry; how poetry for children is read.

1979   *Moon-Bells and Other Poems* by Ted Hughes
JOHN WAIN, ALAN TUCKER & AIDAN CHAMBERS
1979 M 63-79   Nine books discussed. Highly commended: Charles Causley's anthology, *The Puffin Book of Salt-Sea Verse*, and Elizabeth Jennings's collection, *After the Ark*.
  1979 S 169-71   Stephen Corrin objects to the Signal Poetry Award being given to Ted Hughes; Alan Tucker responds.

1980   No award made
AIDAN CHAMBERS
1980 M 67-9   Eight books discussed. Reissues of earlier books the only notable poetry books of the year.
  1980 S 177   Mary O'Neill objects to the Signal Poetry Award not being made; recommends *The Children's Book of Comic Verse*.

1981   No award made
MARGARET MEEK & PETER HUNT
1981 M 67-75   Nine books discussed. Books for teachers—Sandy Brownjohn's *Does It Have to Rhyme?* and Kenneth Koch's *Rose, Where Did You Get That Red?*—noted.

1982 *You Can't Catch Me!* by Michael Rosen & Quentin Blake
PETER HUNT & MARGARET MEEK
1982 M 63-72   Eleven books discussed. Highly commended: Roger McGough's anthology *Strictly Private.*

1983 *The Rattle Bag* edited by Seamus Heaney & Ted Hughes
MARGARET MEEK & NEIL PHILIP
1983 M 59-71   Fourteen books discussed. Highly commended: Charles Causley's anthology *The Sun, Dancing.*

1984 *Sky in the Pie* by Roger McGough
NEIL PHILIP & MARGARET MEEK
1984 M 67-80   Fifteen books discussed. Highly commended: *Quick, Let's Get Out of Here* by Michael Rosen; *Please Mrs Butler* by Allan Ahlberg.

1985 *What is the Truth? A Farmyard Fable for the Young*
by Ted Hughes
NEIL PHILIP & ANTHEA BELL
1985 M 71-85   Sixteen books discussed.
    1985 S 189-90   Mary Hillier objects to the Signal Poetry Award articles; Neil Philip responds substantially.
    1986 J 64-6   Morag Styles agrees with Mary Hillier, and goes on to emphasize that children can write poetry.
    1986 M 142-3   Neil Philip responds to Morag Styles's reaction to Mary Hillier's objection to NP's Signal Poetry Award article.

1986 *Song of the City* by Gareth Owen
ANTHEA BELL & BRIAN MORSE
1986 M 71-85   Nineteen books discussed. Highly commended: Naomi Lewis's anthology *Messages*, Fiona Waters's anthology *Golden Apples.*

1987 *Early in the Morning* by Charles Causley
ANTHEA BELL & BRIAN MORSE
1987 M 79-96   Twenty books discussed. Special mention: Christopher Logue's anthology *The Children's Book of Children's Rhymes.*

1988 *Boo to a Goose* by John Mole
BRIAN MORSE & JAN MARK
1988 M 95-112   Seventeen books discussed. Special mention:

Raymond Wilson's *Daft Davy*; Anne Harvey's anthology *In Time of War*. Brian Morse recaps his three years as award selector.

1989   *When I Dance* by James Berry
JAN MARK & AIDAN CHAMBERS
1989 M 75-92   Twenty-two books discussed. Highly commended: *Come on into My Tropical Garden* by Grace Nichols.

Ten Years of the Signal Poetry Award   NANCY CHAMBERS
1989 M 93-7   A survey and summing-up of the award's first decade.

1990   *Heard it in the Playground* by Allan Ahlberg
JAN MARK & PETER HOLDING
1990 M 87-103   Seventeen books discussed. Highly commended: *Manifold Manor* by Philip Gross.

1991   *This Poem Doesn't Rhyme* edited by Gerard Benson
PETER HOLDING & JAN MARK
1991 M 71-86   Sixteen titles discussed. Highly commended: *Picnic on the Moon* by Brian Morse.

1992   *Shades of Green* edited by Anne Harvey
GERARD BENSON, STEPHEN BICKNELL
& JENNIFER WILSON
1992 M 79-94   Twenty titles discussed. Special mention: Russell Hoban's *The Pedalling Man*.

1993   *Two's Company* by Jackie Kay
DIANA HENDRY, STEPHEN BICKNELL
& JENNIFER WILSON
1993 M 71-93   Thirty-four titles discussed. Highly commended: Gerard Benson's *The Magnificent Callisto* and Matthew Sweeney's *The Flying Spring Onion*.

1994   *The All-Nite Café* by Philip Gross
JENNIFER WILSON, STEPHEN BICKNELL
& NANCY CHAMBERS
1994 M 79-85   Seventeen books discussed.

Poems Published in *Signal*

The Old People; The Thrush; Thoughts about Darwin
three poems by JOAN AIKEN 1990 J 42-4.
**Whispers: Song for Bethnal Green Museum of
Childhood** TESSA ROSE CHESTER 1993 M 131-3.
On a Swing Seat THOMAS A. CLARK 1984 S 172.
Poems THOMAS A. CLARK 1992 J 12, 13.
The Great War in Pictures HUGH CRAGO 1991 S 195-7.
Leonine KEVIN CROSSLEY-HOLLAND 1986 J 42-3.
Natalya Dressing; Mother N.
two poems by ADÈLE GERAS 1991 J 33-4.
Animals Don't Smile JOHN GORDON 1987 J 31.
Quick-change Artists JOHN GORDON 1989 J 3.
Unfair, Unfair JAN MARK 1987 M 116.
The Regretful Philosopher Apologizes to His Cat
JOHN MOLE 1989 M 127.
By the Sound of It; Hop Frog JOHN MOLE 1994 J 17-18.
**Birthday Poem for Paul Turner, 13, E.S.N.; Holiday:
Last Evening; Night in School** three poems by BRIAN MORSE
1971 M 62-4.
**Too Much Story; One of Our Rubbers is Missing; Alice
and the Frog; The Blackbird** four poems by BRIAN MORSE
1986 S 188-92.
Days at School GARETH OWEN 1991 S 169-70.
Discussion Group, Allotments, Clifton Down
three poems by ALAN TUCKER 1971 J 24-7.
The Apple People ALAN TUCKER 1973 J 37.
At Kuala Lipis ALAN TUCKER 1984 S 171.
Mrs Andersen's Butterfly; Mrs Andersen's Story
two poems by ALAN TUCKER 1986 M 118-21.
Birthday JOHN WAIN 1984 S 169-70.

The annotations are arranged chronologically by publication date in *Signal*.

Eleanor Graham MARGARET CLARK
1972 S 91-6   When Eleanor Graham agreed to start the first children's fiction paperback list—for Penguin in 1940—her experience in the 1930s as a pioneer bookseller and as a reviewer in *The Sunday Times* and *The Junior Bookshelf* informed her choice for Puffin Story books: not the standard favourites, but the best of the new books being published. She handed over to Kaye Webb in 1961. Graham, interviewed, also refers to her simultaneous work as editor for Methuen where her special pride was in editing Cynthia Harnett and Stephanie Plowman.

The Puffin Years ELEANOR GRAHAM
1973 S 115-22   Eleanor Graham, the first editor of Puffin for Penguin, writes of the burgeoning of talent in the 1930s and her agreement with Allen Lane in 1940 to publish in paperback 'the best of the *new* classics of the new generation'. She speaks of (hardback) publishers' indignation when approached for paperback rights, of an attempt to 'translate' Will James's *Smoky* into good English, of writing prefaces to classics, of booksellers' reluctance to sell Puffins energetically, about 'original' Puffin anthologies. She describes how she picked Dorothy Edwards and Leila Berg from 'a sackful of manuscripts' the BBC sent to her as Methuen editor, discusses some early information and biography books—and her own *Story of Jesus*.

The Adult-eration of Children's Books ELAINE MOSS
1974 M 65-9   Has the establishment of separate departments for children's books in publishing houses made children's publishing more sophisticated and less child-oriented? Critical acclaim goes to the complex and literary teenage novel (e.g. Alan Garner's *The Owl Service*), possibly at the expense of stories for the middle years, which should be the focus for editors (and reviewers).

Notes from across the North Sea KARI SCHEI   *See page 126.*

A China Diary: Canton; A China Diary: Peking
MARGARET CLARK   *See page 127.*

A Personal Philosophy of Publishing for Children
MARNI HODGKIN
1985 J 44-59 A Sidney Robbins Memorial Lecture. The retired editor
of Macmillan Children's Books reflects on her experiences in New
York in the 1940s and London in the 1960s and 1970s. She speaks of
the positive aspects of publishing for children—speaking to minds that
are forming, the diversity (editing, copy-editing, illustration commis-
sioning), publishing to a 'double audience'—and of the problems
associated with censorship, racism, language, and the famous author for
adults who submits a hopeless story for children. She believes children's
books must present a balance of the world-as-it-is and the world-as-
we-would-like-it-to-be, that hope is an essential ingredient.

A Man of Letters JUDY TAYLOR
1988 M 79-94 Michael Harvey—'a designer who happens to use lettering'—talks to Judy Taylor about his lifelong interest in drawing and
jazz and how the discovery of Eric Gill's *Autobiography* directed his
enthusiasm towards lettering and book design. Many illustrations of
'Harvey' book jackets are included as well as his *Signal* logo ('It was a
lovely job to do. The lower case "g" is my favourite letter. It has such a
good shape, with its bold ear and its long tail') and Thimble Press
Bookguide covers.

Work in Progress on *Intimate Leaves from a Designer's Notebook* JOHN RYDER
A series of inserts in *Signal* by the eminent typographic and book
designer. May 1989: Introduction; September 1989: 'The Last Letter';
January 1990: 'The Typography Critic'; May 1990: 'Extra-Dimensional
Book Design'.

Lessons in Publishing MARGARET CLARK
1990 J 45-50 The education of an editor in the 1950s. Margaret Clark
recalls her job as 'dogsbody' at Penguin's Harmondsworth offices
where she was able to observe every aspect of publishing as a business,
and her apprenticeship years with Eleanor Graham, founder of the
Puffin list. The exacting standards in language (Alan Glover), design
and illustration (Hans Schmoller) and author/publisher relations (Noel
Carrington) together with Eleanor Graham's experience in children's
books are nostalgically remembered; though Sir Allen Lane's management skills are not revered, his enthusiasm is.

Children's Publishing in the 1930s: Memoirs of an American in London GRACE HOGARTH

1990 J 51-63   Fresh from the lively US children's book scene—peopled largely by enthusiastic women—a young editor arrives at the Oxford University Press in London where Mr L'Estrange and Mr Ely ('Herbert Strang') were producing popular stories for boys, where Edward Ardizzone had presented his first 'Little Tim' for publication (by offset photolithography, a new process, in New York), and where Big Books and Annuals were all that the market wanted to handle. Grace Hogarth compares UK librarians' attitude to publishers with the US, the British Library's attitude to children's books with that of the Library of Congress. Also discussed: Leslie Brooke.

The Author and the Editor: The Inaugural Patrick Hardy Lecture JILL PATON WALSH & JOHN ROWE TOWNSEND

1990 J 64-82   In conversation, two authors delve away to discover the essence of a good editor—to bring forth the best possible book; to copy-edit with sensitivity, intelligence and skill; and to build a list with flavour. In all of these areas Patrick Hardy excelled as well as in offering his authors the essential: friendship. The authors recognize that with the advent of large corporations in publishing the days of the editor-author relationship are numbered.

Picking Up the Book JOHN GOLDTHWAITE

1990 S 163-76   '... here we are, a century down the pike in accumulated wisdom and still depriving children of a sense of discovery and empowerment by continuing to convert the art of their literature into the art of the limited edition.' A broadside fired from the US at the uninviting (to children) nature of much of modern publishing; children's book design should be 'culinary' (seducing the appetite), not decorative; fine art in picture books reduces the child to a role that is 'virtually superfluous as a participant'—like TV; fairy tales are over-colourfully illustrated—line illustration is preferable; and a plea for the return of the 'pile it up, crowd it in' anthology, 'a magic attic'.

Introduction to *Signal* 70 MARGARET CLARK

1993 J 3-4   *Signal* 70 was edited by Margaret Clark and consisted of reminiscences (quite different from official records) of publishing and reading in the years 1930-1970. Will the microchip make libraries, so important in the years under consideration, redundant? The cheapness of books (Penguin, Everyman, World Classics) is referred to time and again in the 'reader' articles.

Penguins in the Early Fifties: A Personal Memory
DAVID HERBERT
1993 J 28-35   The idealism of those who worked at Penguin in the 1950s believing the paperback revolution to be part of modernism, socialism and a new world thirsty for knowledge after World War II—described by an editor of the time. 'Marketing would have been a fifties dirty word.'

A Puffin Illustrator of the Forties   SHEILA JACKSON
1993 J 37-45   Despite the War Noel Carrington at Penguin was able to produce the Puffin Picture Books series of information books for children. Sheila Jackson had learned the art of lithography at art school and was therefore sent along by her tutor, Clarke Hutton, to Carrington. She describes the arduous work of lithographic illustration and her own and other artists' contributions to the series.

A Children's Book Publisher of the Fifties
ROBIN DENNISTON
1993 J 46-52   The author was Children's Editor at Collins from 1953 to 1959, succeeding Pamela Whitlock and benefiting from the period when Billy Collins decided to 'drive Collins up-market—often kicking and shrieking'. Buckeridge, Streatfeild, the Pullein-Thompsons came on to the Collins list at the same time that Oxford University Press and other publishers were also defying their sales departments and going for quality.

Whatever Happened to Little Oleg?: Brockhampton
Press in the Sixties   ANTONY KAMM
1993 J 53-66   Antony Kamm surveys the wide variety of publishing, all of it for children (apart from Margery Fisher's *Intent Upon Reading*—a seminal critical work for adults in the field), undertaken by the Brockhampton Press in Leicester—part of the Hodder Group. Mary Mouse comic strip (on off-cuts during paper rationing) was succeeded in the sixties by the huge success of Asterix, picture books like the 'Pilgrim's Farm' and 'Andy Pandy' series and Gumdrop for the very young, Brock Books for early readers. Picture Reference Books for older children were joined by quality literature (Causley, Treece) and picture books (Keeping). Because the firm had its own paperback list (Knight) it could be said to be the first 'vertical' publisher.

RESEARCH

The annotations are arranged chronologically by publication date in *Signal*.

Cushla and Her Books DOROTHY BUTLER *See page 48.*

Carol, Cushla and Rebecca VIRGINIA LOWE *See page 48.*

Children's Book Research in Britain PETER HUNT
1978 J 12-15 With the empirical nature of much book reviewing and with many disciplines (as in *The Cool Web*, review on page 60) using children's books as base material Peter Hunt conducts a survey of research in children's literature being carried out in the UK and, giving results, concludes that there is much to be done if it is to establish firm foundations.

The Children's Literature Association M.P. ESMONDE
1978 S 163-4 A description of the (American) Children's Literature Association's purpose and publications includes the Awards Committee's citation for its choice of Aidan Chambers's 'The Reader in the Book' (see page 60) for 1978 to receive its first award, made for 'excellence in the field of literary criticism'.

International Exchange? STUART AMOR *See page 126.*

The Mayne Game: An Experiment in Response
PETER HUNT *See page 41.*

The Great Hunt JUDY TAYLOR
1986 M 86-91 An editor-turned-sleuth unearths source material for a life of Beatrix Potter.

Rrtr's 'Strbk': A Report from the Academy
PETER F. NEUMEYER
1987 S 178-85 A send-up analysis of an imaginary storybook, the only

children's book published in Kwzkn. 'A degree of broadly limned directness as well as Bayreuthian echoes' is noted as is the present location of 'this totally unprepossessing spiral notebook: in the International Youth Library behind the Karl May pseudo-erotica'.

Questions about Elinor HELEN McCLELLAND
1988 M 123-32   A researcher describes her frustrations in tracking down relevant facts about the life of Elinor Brent-Dyer; she also discusses Brent-Dyer's attitude to class and religion, coming to the conclusion that inconsistency was 'perhaps her most striking characteristic'.

Little Anna and Big Anna ANNA CRAGO
1994 S 177-81   The child as raw material for adult researchers (her parents, Hugh and Maureen Crago) into child response to children's literature. Anna Crago, now adult, looks back at her childhood experience as the subject of her parents' study without recrimination.

'What are you Writing?': The Parent-Observer at Home
VIRGINIA LOWE
1994 S 182-93   A parent researcher reports on her children's responses to books and to her role as recorder of these responses.

Books about Children's Books SHEILA RAY
An annual feature surveying the previous year's output of publications about children's-literature subjects. Sheila Ray began compiling this feature for *The Signal Selection* in 1987; it appeared in the *Selection* for 1988 and 1989, and transferred to *Signal* in May 1991.

Books about Children's Books 1990 1991 M 120-8.
Books about Children's Books 1991 1992 M 128-37.
Books about Children's Books 1992 1993 M 115-30.
Books about Children's Books 1993 1994 M 132-40.

Notebook PELORUS
An in-house column of informal comment on current subjects of interest. Each column consists of discrete items.

1972 S 128-9   Margery Fisher, *Matters of Fact*; Fred Inglis, *The Imagery of Power: A Critique of Advertising*; Catherine Sinclair, *Holiday House*; picture books, *Father Fox's Pennyrhymes*.

1973 J 52-4   Philippa Pearce, *What the Neighbours Did*; Marcus Crouch, *The Nesbit Tradition*; Maurice Sendak; reviewing; *Watership Down*, Richard Adams.

1973 M 108-11   reviewing; racism; Russell Hoban, for adults/for children.

1973 S 162-4   *Children Are People*, Janet Hill, librarianship; Raymond Briggs, *Father Christmas*; Nicholas Brennan, *Olaf's Incredible Machine*; picture books, Dr Seuss, *The Lorax*; *When the Land Lay Waste*, Neils Jensen.

1975 J 146-8   Robert Cormier, *The Chocolate War*; Janet and Allan Ahlberg, *The Brick Street Boys*; Ivan Southall, *Journey of Discovery;* Robert Westall, *The Machine-Gunners*; Charles Causley.

1976 M 96-9   John Gordon; school bookshops; Jan Mark, *Thunder and Lightnings*; books in school, the Oldmeadows.

1976 S 148-50   *The Stone Book*, Alan Garner; Samuel Hynes, *The Auden Generation;* censorship, teenage books

1979 J 54-8   Dorothy Butler, *Cushla and Her Books;* Humphrey Carpenter, *The Inklings*, John Wain; typographic readability; Mary Rayner, Raymond Briggs, *The Snowman, Fungus the Bogeyman*.

1979 M 109   Letter from Jill Bennett responding to the comments on typographic readability. It was her quoting from *Cushla* that led *Signal*'s editor to invite her to compile a list of picture books she used in helping children learn to read. In 1996 Jill Bennett's Signal Bookguide *Learning to Read with Picture Books* is in its fourth edition.

American Dispatch JOHN DONOVAN
Current events viewed by the Executive Director of the US Children's Book Council in New York City. Each column consists of discrete items.

1973 M 65-8   Censorship; children's literature centre; Newbery Medal; awards; Randall Jarrell's *Snow-White and the Seven Dwarfs*, illustrated by Nancy Ekholm Burkert.

1973 S 156-60   National Book Award; Ursula Le Guin; fantasy;

paperback publishing; *Cricket*; Lynd Ward's *The Silver Pony*; wordless picture books.

1974 J 16-20   Publishing concerns; awards; reviewing; differences US/UK; bibliography; *The Juniper Tree*.

1974 M 85-90   Censorship; awards; racism; Raymond Briggs's *Father Christmas*.

1974 S 131-5   Richard Adams's *Watership Down*; publishing; National Book Awards.

1975 J 40-5   Robert Cormier's *The Chocolate War*; controversial books; differences US/UK; awards, booklists, promotion.

1975 M 91-5   Newbery Medal; National Book Award; Virginia Hamilton's *M.C. Higgins, the Great*; Laura Ingalls Wilder Award to Beverly Cleary.

1976 J 40-4   Publishing 'easy readers'; Pierpont Morgan book exhibition; National Book Award.

1976 M 78-82   Whole column devoted to US children's books editors' views on the differences between US and UK publishing.

1976 S 143-7   Racism; political correctness.

1977 J 38-43   Bruno Bettelheim's *The Uses of Enchantment*; fairy tales; Barbara Bader's *American Picturebooks from Noah's Ark to the Beast Within*.

1977 S 111-16   William Steig; John Goldthwaite's 'Notes on the Children's Book Trade'; Robert Cormier's *I am the Cheese*.

1978 M 85-91   Intellectual freedom; censorship; other social issues.

1979 J 3-8   American review editors comment on British-originated children's books.

The American Connection BETSY HEARNE
A reviewer and critic discusses current concerns in the US children's book world.

1980 J 36-41   Is slipping controversial books to the bottom of the reviewing pile the thin end of the censorship wedge?

1980 S 151-9   Application of George Selden's 'one of the most ubiquitous shortcomings in US literature—the premature delivery of fetal ideas' to children's books.

1981 M 91-5   The arrival of a new baby reminds the reviewer of the importance of play in picture books for the very young.

1982 J 38-42   The toy book/mechanical book trend in the US market: how Robert Crowther's *The Most Amazing Alphabet Book* gained itself a *Booklist* (journal of the American Library Association) review despite being a pop-up; advances in board-book design compared with the banality of cloth books; necessity of co-publication.

1982 S 191-5 Guest columnist BARBARA ELLEMAN writes about the publication and reviewing of biblical and religious books for children.

Margaret Meek recommends

1981 J 60-2 *The Foundations of Literacy* by Don Holdaway; *Traditional Romance and Tale—How Stories Mean* by Anne Wilson; *Child and Tale: The Origins of Interest* by André Favat.

1982 J 50-1 *Reading Blake's 'Songs'* by Zachary Leader; *The Impact of Victorian Children's Fiction* by J.S. Bratton; *Learning Through Interaction: The Study of Language Development* by Gordon Wells et al.

1986 M 141-2 . *Literacy in Theory and Practice* by Brian Street; *The Social Context of Literacy* by Kenneth Levine; *Women Writing about Men* by Jane Miller.

1987 J 74 *Actual Minds, Possible Worlds* by Jerome Bruner; *Culture, Communication, Cognition: Vygotskyan Perspectives* by J.V. Wertsch.

From the Editor 1984 S 127-8; 1985 S 193-5

SOCIAL ISSUES

The subjects of class, race, religion, gender, handicap, death, conservation, politics—ideology generally—arise specifically and inevitably throughout the pages of *Signal*; indeed, it would be possible to classify most articles under, or cross-reference them to, this Social Issues heading. See especially in **American Dispatch, The American Connection**, the sections on teenage reading and translations.

Accepting the Eleanor Farjeon Award JANET HILL *See page 95.*

Through Literature to Life? A National Book League Conference

1973 M 102-7 Should literature be 'useful'? Can it legitimately be considered as a social tool? An Rutgers van der Loeff felt children could be prepared through literature for the shocks life can bring them, but cautioned against going 'too far'. Catherine Storr stressed the power of fantasy as important in getting ideas across to readers. Nina Bawden felt that children identified with the emotional rather than the social land-scape, and that adventure stories allowed them to test themselves vicariously in situations. Robert Leeson spoke of the lessons authors could learn from the dynamic techniques of comic strip.

Boom ROBERT LEESON
1974 J 3 -9 A plea for the widening of the range of children's books which, even in a boom period, remain the preserve of the middle class. Enid Blyton's simple story lines and unpretentious vocabulary could be used to convey more worthwhile sentiments in novels for the middle years, for whom there is a dearth of good new material. Reviewing should be frequent, regular and informed, and can be properly under-taken by children on a serious level.
1974 M 106-7   Reactions from two publishers, Susan Dickinson (Collins) and J.J. Curle (Macdonald); RL replies.

The Other Award ANDREW MANN
1975 S 142-5 The aims of the Other Award: first, to underline the fact that a growing number of writers are concerning themselves with social issues; second, to encourage a critical approach that encompasses all the elements of a book; third, to choose three books for the annual award with no outright winner and to declare reasons for the choices. Also discussed: Children's Rights Workshop.

What Were We Arguing About? ROBERT LEESON
1976 M 55-63   An author committed to the idea that literature for children should reflect the lives of the whole society, not just one sec-tion of it, believes that progress has been made: girls 'now move with a freedom and decisiveness' in novels. In writing the history of a Drake voyage in novel form Leeson discovered that the slaves played a big role in their own fight for freedom (*'Maroon Boy*); he speaks, too, of the change in school stories from the private to the comprehensive (*The Third Class Genie*), of black characters and of 'golden rules' for writing for the children of the 1970s. Are these any different from those of the more conventional children's literature?

Stories for Life: A Book Exhibition GRACE HALLWORTH
1981 S 182-93   Hertfordshire Schools Library Service mounts a book exhibition for a conference of voluntary and official organizations (in-cluding psychiatrists, social workers, playgroup leaders) to show the range of interests related to the development of children. An explana-

tory paragraph precedes the list of books in each section.

The Child's Changing Story AIDAN CHAMBERS *See page 63.*

The Secret Seven vs *The Twits*: **Cultural Clash or Cosy Combination?** CHARLES SARLAND
1983 S 155-71 The author looks at Blyton's conservatism and Dahl's subversive ethos in an article that is concerned with the political ideology of both writers (and how children observe or fail to notice this). Dahl's 'fascist' order, Blyton's sexism and narrow class attitudes come under the microscope. The integral role of Quentin Blake's illustrations in Dahl's stories is also discussed. Reference made to work of Gérard Genette and Roland Barthes.

The Civilizing Process in Fairy Tales ANNE WILSON
See page 122.

Translator's Notebook: Delicate Matters ANTHEA BELL
See page 128.

Second Impression: *Tales out of School* by Geoffrey Trease
PETER HOLLINDALE
1987 J 3-11 Geoffrey Trease's polemical *Tales out of School* (1949, 2nd ed. 1964) professionalized the domain of children's literature, challenged the conformist bias and suggested that the writer for children was like 'the parent and schoolmaster' (i.e. having a responsibility for the development of social attitudes in young people). Hollindale sees this as controversial: if schools are exhorted to watch the ideology of books in their libraries (as has happened in the intervening decades) freedom of expression and thought may be threatened.

Ideology and the Children's Book PETER HOLLINDALE
1988 J 3-22 Ideology is a living thing because it is part of us. It is present in a children's book in three ways: the social, political or moral belief of the writer; the writer's unexamined assumptions; the captivity of mind we undergo by living where and when we do. However, the author's ideology does not pour itself into an empty receptacle; surface didacticism leaves many children 'with their own divergent ideology intensified by resentful bemusement'. Ideology is inseparable from language: national *and* local literature are important. For the 'child' person who wants books 'kids will like . . . the "kids" are a Kid, who is sexless

116

but female, colourless but black, classless but proletarian'. (Recipient of the year's Children's Literature Association Criticism Award.)

Second Impression: *Tellers of Tales* by Roger Lancelyn Green
PETER HUNT
1988 M 142-9   *Tellers of Tales* (1946, 1953, 1965) in recommending books for the older child made no distinction between writers for adults and writers for children; lucid and urbane, it greatly influenced the style and approach of children's book criticism in the mid twentieth century. It is concerned with Green as a reader and the book as an absolute. 'It may be disturbing that books and meanings are no longer stable entities, and that values shift along so many axes, but the Arcadia from which Green wrote is only available to us if we reject the world as it is.' Though Trease and Leeson are ideologically left-wing and Inglis perceptibly right (despite his liberal-humanist label), Green and his heirs (like Carpenter) accept the status quo of their periods and are therefore far from neutral.

The Last Days in the Old Home   HUGH CRAGO   *See page 92.*

The Darkening of the Green   PETER HOLLINDALE
1990 J 3-19   The green seeds planted by his teenage reading of 'faction' by 'Romany' and 'Nomad' and of Kenneth Allsop's *Silver Flame* have darkened in Peter Hollindale in maturity: homocentricity in our thinking is destroying our planet but literature—especially children's literature, which has led the way—can help to reverse our direction. Mowgli, the Robinsonades 'disturb the complacent illusion of expectedness by which we mostly live', but Lucy Boston's *A Stranger at Green Knowe* best expresses the need for respect for the biological space of other creatures if we are to survive. Hollindale also looks at current teenage 'Holocaust' fiction.

The Interpretation of Parables   TED HUGHES
1992 S 147-52   Ted Hughes replies to the Kent county councillor who condemned Hughes's story 'How the Polar Bear Became' as unsuitable for use 'in a multicultural society' by considering the nature of parable, its wholeness, its potential for being internalized by children as a map for real life. He talks about *The Iron Man* in this context. 'To read ['How the Polar Bear Became'] as in any way "racist" because of Polar Bear's whiteness is to condemn it with the blindness that it is meant to immunize the reader against.'

Biggles Goes to the Cleaners ANTHONY E. GREAVES
1993 S 176–83 The Biggles series by W.E. Johns, reissued in 1993 with minor alterations in deference to 'political correctness', is so shot through with jingoistic and class assumptions that the implicit 1940s messages of superiority remain.

Rupert in Space and Time HUGH CRAGO *See page 69.*

Trying to Be Good ALAN TUCKER *See page 81.*

TEENAGE READING

The annotations are arranged chronologically by publication date in *Signal.*

A Book is a Book is a Book
ROSEMARY MANNING *See page 43.*

The Catcher in the Steppes: Soviet Adolescent Fiction in Translation CELIA BOYD *See page 124.*

The Bare Pebble: The Novels of John Gordon
EDWARD BLISHEN *See page 38.*

Growing Pains: A Survey of Honor Arundel's Novels
CELIA BOYD *See page 33.*

Dreams Must Explain Themselves URSULA LE GUIN
See page 39.

The Chaos and the Track ROBERT WESTALL
1978 J 3–11 Tracks are necessary to keep animals (and humans) sane. At sixteen the adolescent finds the familiar tracks of childhood and early teenage (family, school, gang) challenged; entering a world where chaos looms he is bewildered and likely to become addicted to pop music, bikes, etc. Sixteen is, therefore, a difficult age to publish for.

The Novels of Molly Holden ROGER ALMA *See page 39.*

An Interview with Alan Garner AIDAN CHAMBERS
See page 37.

How Real Do You Want Your Realism? ROBERT WESTALL
1979 J 34-46 Robert Westall begins by comparing Laurie Lee's evocations of childhood with James Kirkup's. Westall's first novel, *The Machine-Gunners*, was a success because he re-created himself aged twelve for his son aged twelve—and that is the way adults should write for children. He regards himself as having been seduced from that realism (towards fantasy) by the adult nostalgia for childhood of publishers, teachers, reviewers. He explores children's fascination with death and horror. He reveres the work of Alan Garner, in which sex and class realism are germane, and of Jill Paton Walsh, whose *Emperor's Winding Sheet* invites the reader into a story about dissolution.

An Interview with Robert Cormier AIDAN CHAMBERS
See page 35.

After the Gate WILLIAM CORLETT *See page 96.*

Whatever Happened to Jan Mark? PETER HUNT *See page 40.*

Images of Adolescence SUSAN THOMPSON
1981 J, M 37-59,108-125 A dissertation on teenage and on teenage fiction, its current and past state, its realism (or lack of it), its tendency towards didacticism. If fiction has a function in adults' lives, then teenage fiction should play the same role in the lives of adolescents; failure (often) to represent adult life and its problems or to reflect the positive aspects of adolescence alongside its emotional swings is remarked upon, as is the market for teenage literature (largely adults on behalf of teenagers) which, the writer believes, partially governs the genre. A small number of carefully chosen titles illustrates her points about sexuality, identity and didacticism.

The Slow Art of John Gordon EDWARD BLISHEN *See page 38.*

The Novels of Robert C. O'Brien BRIAN MORSE *See page 41.*

Blume's Adolescents: Coming of Age in Limbo
LYNNE HAMILTON *See page 34.*

In Defence of Jan: Love and Betrayal in
The Owl Service and *Red Shift* VICTOR WATSON *See page 38.*

All of a Tremble to See His Danger AIDAN CHAMBERS
See page 78.

Easy Connections: **Emotional Truth and**
Fictional Gratification HUGH CRAGO *See page 34.*

An Interview with Nadia Wheatley
AGNES NIEUWENHUIZEN *See page 44.*

Attack of the Teenage Horrors: Theme and Meaning in
Popular Series Fiction CHARLES SARLAND
1994 J 49-62 Various aspects of the Point Horror series discussed: the authors' use of the thriller formula to play out conflicts of friendship, loyalty and trust, speaking from the heart of the teenage culture and indicating the limits of behaviour that must not be transgressed. Always the issue to be resolved is that of the outsider in a milieu that is invariably white, middle-class, rich, hedonistic. The series is entertainment, not a religious tract: teenagers don't want to 'believe' ... 'they want to observe and learn'. The format and covers of the paperback series and the publisher's marketing techniques also commented upon.

Reading New Books PAULINE THOMAS
1992 M 138-42 Review article on 1991 novels by Jan Mark, Anne Fine, Jon Blake, Philip Gross, Adèle Geras, Pam Conrad, Berlie Doherty, and other writers for adolescents.

Revenge of the Teenage Horrors: Pleasure, Quality
and Canonicity in (and out of) Popular Series Fiction
CHARLES SARLAND
1994 M 113-31 Are the National Curriculum and reading for pleasure two opposed canons? Adult critics look at formula teenage fiction such as the Point Horror series (see above) with the eye of experience and dismiss it as trash—but teenagers are reading critically about the future they may be entering. Twelve-year-olds discuss the series with Sarland, showing appreciation of structure, situation, pace, character.

TRADITIONAL TALES

The annotations are arranged chronologically by publication date in *Signal*.

The Cinderella Story 1724-1919 IRENE WHALLEY *See page 76.*

The Simple Truth ERIK CHRISTIAN HAUGAARD
1973 M 69-73 The translator of Hans C. Andersen gives a pen portrait of Andersen's simple charm and his striving to understand the changes technology would bring (he called the machine 'Master Bloodless', for instance); and he describes the problems of translating from Danish into English and the temptation to use words that express the translator's rather than the author's viewpoint.

Andersen Complete ALAN TUCKER
1975 J 12-17 Calling Hans C. Andersen 'the first modern writer for children ... combining classical prose with romantic idealism', Alan Tucker goes on to compare previous translations with Erik Haugaard's: 'with Haugaard you always feel you are reading Andersen and no one but Andersen'. *The Complete Fairy Tales and Stories* gives us 'not a fantasy world, but a microcosm reflecting ... our everyday surroundings'.

Folk Tales for Children in the Soviet Union
STUART AMOR *See page 124.*

'Origins' from *A History of Storytelling* ARTHUR RANSOME
See page 42.

Rumcajs, A Modern Fairy-Tale Hero STUART AMOR
See page 126.

K.M. Briggs, Novelist ELAINE MOSS *See page 34.*

'Snow White': One Child's Response in a Natural Setting
MAUREEN CRAGO
1980 J 42-56 From the age of three to the age of six, Anna Crago

responds to various picture-book or illustrated versions of 'Snow-White'; the aspects of story frequently referred to over the years (charted by her mother) are the stepmother, the poisoned fruit, Snow-White's beauty.

Cinderella's Many Guises: A Look at Early Sources and Recent Versions NEIL PHILIP

1980 S 130-46 A comprehensive study of the many versions, worldwide, of the Cinderella story, with Charles Perrault cast as the villain of the piece. The fairy tale, a set form of the story, diminishes the folk tale, the infinite variety of which in its oral presentation is its strength.

Magical Thought in Story ANNE WILSON *See page 74.*

A New Arabian Nights ANNE WILSON

1983 J 26-9 Geraldine McCaughrean's *One Thousand and One Arabian Nights* is compared, in this extended review, with older versions and is declared an excellent selection from the tales, told in language which is 'a constant excitement'.

Talking Pictures: A New Look at *Hansel and Gretel* JANE DOONAN *See page 85.*

Fireside Tales of the Traveller Children DUNCAN WILLIAMSON

1984 J 3-11 A Scottish traveller writes of the importance of storytelling in traveller culture, the grading of the stories he tells to suit the age of the listener, the lessons taught by stories and the threat to the culture by radio and television.

Dr Bettelheim and Enchantment NICHOLAS TUCKER

1984 J 33-41 Review article on Bruno Bettelheim's *The Uses of Enchantment* finds the author's blanket use of 'the child' as responder to the tales unacceptable, since children differ from one another. Bettelheim's selective approach to fairy tales (to suit his own theories) is also criticized.

The Civilizing Process in Fairy Tales ANNE WILSON

1984 M 81-7 In a review article on Jack Zipes' *The Trials and Tribulations of Little Red Riding Hood* and *Fairy Tales and the Art of Subversion* Anne Wilson raises objections to the Marxist and feminist views on fairy tales, believing that a superficial approach inspired by ideological concerns can miss both the fun and the deeper significance of the 'magic' (see page 74) tale. Traditional tales are constantly rewritten, 'their purpose being to civilize children' according to the values of their time. Feminists fail to understand that the heroines of 'Beauty and the Beast' and 'The Goose Girl' are encountering their feelings and dealing with them.

Two Artists Telling Tales JANE DOONAN *See page 87.*

Translator's Notebook: On Approaching the Traditional Tale ANTHEA BELL *See page 128.*

The Black Rabbit JOHN GOLDTHWAITE *See page 65.*

Who Does Snow-White Look At? HUGH CRAGO *See page 90.*

Enter Fairy Godmother ... HILDA ELLIS DAVIDSON
1991 S 171-8 The various guises of the fairy godmother explored. The Greek Kourotrophos (nursing mother), the animal helpers, the supernatural fairy godmothers of Perrault and Grimm (and their Freudian and Jungian interpretations) are discussed, as well as the recurrence of spinning in the stories and the fertility connection.

Reading New Books MARY STEELE *See page 72.*

TRANSLATION, INTERNATIONALISM & NATIONAL LITERATURES

The annotations are arranged chronologically by publication date in *Signal*.

How I Became a Writer KORNEI CHUKOVSKY *See page 35.*

Re-viewing Reiner Zimnik, or 'Don't Mind Me! I'm Happy!' NINA DANISCHEWSKY *See page 45.*

The Catcher in the Steppes: Soviet Adolescent Fiction
in Translation CELIA BOYD
1972 J 13-30 The publication in Russian of J.D. Salinger's *Catcher in the Rye* combined with the softening of political attitudes brings the teenage novel into Soviet literature in the 1960s. Frolov, Balter and Aksenov wrote fiction in which the adolescent's personal problems in coming to terms with society were portrayed in novels in which Communism was not preached but simply assumed to be part of life. The novels are reviewed. Paul Zindel's debt to Salinger also discussed.

Skip-rope Rhymes: Some International Variations
FRANCELIA BUTLER *See page 99.*

The Simple Truth ERIK CHRISTIAN HAUGAARD
See page 121.

Chiyoko Nakatani ELAINE MOSS *See page 87.*

Children's Books of Today: A Scandinavian Seminar
KARI SCHEI
1974 S 136-40 At a Scandinavian seminar on children's quality literature for seven- to twelve-year-olds the delegates divide into two camps on the subject of realism: left-wing writers who believe children's literature should be an active agent in the class struggle, and moderates who want a social but not socialistic children's literature. The translation of Finnish books into Swedish, and standards for judging children's literature also discussed.

Andersen Complete ALAN TUCKER *See page 121.*

Folk Tales for Children in the Soviet Union STUART AMOR
1975 J 46-52 The battle of the folk tale in the Soviet Union, a country rich in oral material but one in which, even before the Revolution, sides were taken (Toll and Lensky versus Tolstoy and Dostoevsky) about its educational value. After 1917 the debate became one of social realism versus the imagination (championed by Kornei Chukovsky). The diverse ethnic groups which formed the Soviet Union could be introduced to one another through their folk tales. Lenin became a nationwide folk hero when in due course the folk tale was widely used as socialist propaganda.

Robinsonades: The J.A. Ahlstrand Collection
MARGIT HOFFMAN *See page 57.*

Will It Travel Well? PATRICIA CRAMPTON
1975 M 75-80 A translator describes the importance of reading books from other cultures and suggests two categories that should be chosen for translation: books in which the background is strong; books which fill a gap in the literature of the translating country. The translator must be prepared to transmit the intentions of the original as well as the style: but what is the translator's duty faced, in the course of an otherwise good novel, with a sudden burst of Marxist ideology? The social issues in Swedish children's literature are commented upon.

Swedish Children's Books in Britain PETER GRAVES
1975 S 137-41 The author describes his frustrations in his attempt to make a bibliographical survey of Swedish children's books published in Britain 1950-74: reviews are inadequate, criticism less advanced than in Sweden where teachers attend courses in children's literature when in training. Of the literature in translation Graves finds a large number of novels by very few authors—and among publishers an unwillingness to translate Sven Wernström because of his Marxist views.

Muscular Ideology: A Look at Chinese Children's Books
C. S. HANNABUSS
1976 M 68-77 Chinese children's books are ideologically inspired, aiming to integrate the individual into the mass, whereas Western literature celebrates individuality. The latter is, nevertheless, didactic in its own way (the Christian ethic in nineteenth-century writers such as Kingsley, Ballantyne, Marryat, Henty). 'The crucial critical factor which differentiates memorable writing from transient propaganda in fictional guise is the quality . . . in literary and imaginative terms.'

Josef Lada, Illustrator STUART AMOR
1976 S 108-14 The clarity of Joseph Lada's illustrations (for *The Good Soldier Schweik* as well as for numerous Czechoslovakian children's books) bears witness to his early days when his work was published in wide-circulation magazines printed on cheap paper. His drawings of animals with all the characteristics and weaknesses of human beings were an invitation to children to live in harmony with nature.

Notes from across the North Sea KARI SCHEI
1978 J 30-3 The advantages (price, publicity, collectability) of publishing in series weighed against the disadvantages (cult series diminish-
ing the author's individuality, wholesale import) in the small
Norwegian children's book trade. 'In the end we have no readers for
the "special book", no books for the "special reader".' Also discussed:
the international picture book; imported Swedish series; Norwegian
book prizes.

Sven Wernström, Traditionalist and Reformer
PETER GRAVES
1978 M 78-80; 83-4; KARI SCHEI 81-3 The literary adventure
story as a vehicle for left-wing political persuasion in the work of a
Swedish Marxist writer is analysed by a university lecturer, who believes that 'there is no good reason why children should be excluded
from political debate'. Kari Schei, Norwegian librarian, quotes from
Wernström's dicta to demonstrate his didactic intentions and recognizes that accepting the status quo is also political.

Rumcajs, A Modern Fairy-Tale Hero STUART AMOR
1978 S 150-62 The *pohadka* (stories for young children) tradition in
Czechoslovakia and the place of the modern fairy-tale hero Rumcajs
within it. Ctrvrtek's careful choice of names to denote character, his
free use of language, his humour in the tales of the small man up against
larger forces make the written stories even more important than their
TV originals. The modern fairy tale is a release from the inroads of
technology in our lives. A Rumcajs story translated by Amor is
appended.

Children's Books in Translation ANTHEA BELL
1979 J 47-53 A review of *Children's Books in Translation: The Situation
and the Problems* edited by Göte Klingberg, Mary Ørvig and Stuart
Amor, based on the International Research Society for Children's Literature's symposium on the subject.

International Exchange? STUART AMOR
1979 M 103-8 After the fourth symposium of the International
Research Society for Children's Literature Stuart Amor ponders the
meaning of internationalism and emphasizes the importance to conferences of the calibre of individual participants, including their willingness to be frank.

Ten Years of Parcels ANTHEA BELL
1980 J 20-8 A seasoned translator writes about the responsibility of acting as publisher's reader, reporting on foreign submissions as a preliminary to translation. She believes that the elimination of perceived sexism in fairy tales is pointless because in many the girl is the catalyst; she describes being inundated with European novels in which 'drugs, death, pregnancy' abound—though the best of these submissions rise above the label 'sociological novel'; and she gives examples of how the English are represented in novels from other cultures.

A China Diary: Canton; A China Diary: Peking
MARGARET CLARK
1980 M,S 93-106; 160-75 A children's books editor describes her experiences as part of a Book Development Council's mission to exhibit British books in China (some shortcomings in advance preparation are itemized) and to discover how the Chinese book market functions. In Canton she concentrates on bookselling and the shortage of foreign-language books, partly due to currency reasons. In Peking she delves into the People's Republic's publishing methods and visits reading rooms organized by street communes in the absence of any lending libraries so far as she could discover.

The Kurt Maschler Award ELAINE MOSS *See page 47.*

Who Remembers *Elizabeth*? M. NANCY CUTT
1982 S 153-62 Mme Sophie Cottin's *Elizabeth* (Paris 1806) is more than a *roman passionel*—it is a moral work (widely translated and also used as the basis for toy theatre and opera performance) but one of sensibility, offsetting eighteenth-century callousness and rationality.

Learning Without Literature ELAINE MOSS *See page 55.*

Two Artists Telling Tales: Chihiro Iwasaki and Lisbeth Zwerger JANE DOONAN *See page 87.*

Translator's Notebook: The Naming of Names ANTHEA BELL
1985 J 3-11 Reflections on the xenophobic British and on the problems presented by proper names and by rhymes in the process of translation: some brilliant solutions as examples.

Translator's Notebook: On Approaching the Traditional Tale
ANTHEA BELL
1985 S 139-47   Strictly speaking the traditional/folk/fairy tale belongs
to everyone to do with as they please. Yet the translator of Grimm or
Perrault has a duty to be faithful to the text while coping with problems of names (Hänsel und Gretel became Little Hans and Meg in an
early complete Grimm in English), of rhyme and especially of gender.
Snow-White, the Robber Bridegroom tales, and the influence of illustrators are also discussed.

Translator's Notebook: Delicate Matters ANTHEA BELL
1986 J 17-26   The modern translator is faced not only with the ordinary problems of tense, pronouns, and local dialect, but with contemporary sensibilities over sexism and racism. She welcomed the
opportunity to revise her 1960s translation of *Asterix* and recognizes the
need to meet the charges of racism in both *Asterix* and *Tintin*.

A Visit to Japan EILEEN COLWELL *See page 96.*

Wanted—Tove Jansson's Cartoon Books! ANNE WILSON
1987 J 12-23   A plea for editions in English of the Moomin comic
strips. Several examples, with Anne Wilson's translations, provided.

Endpapers 1987 S 210   Anthea Bell recommends Göte Klingberg's
Children's Fiction in the Hands of Translators.

Children's Books in Teacher Education at the University of Sydney
GEOFF WILLIAMS *See page 54.*

I Remember ... ASTRID LINDGREN *See page 40.*

Double Dutch JOKE LINDERS
1989 J 31-8 An overview of the development of children's literature in
the Netherlands—the didacticism of both Protestant and Roman
Catholic texts for children which kept fantasies (*Alice in Wonderland, The
Tale of Peter Rabbit*) untranslated until World War II loosened up the
field. Also covered: current criticism, learning to read, awards, modern
Dutch authors and illustrators who win international acclaim.

Teaching Children's Literature in Canada LISSA PAUL
See page 52.

Tarzan the Incomparable TOVE JANSSON *See page 39.*

Children's Literature in New Zealand: New Initiatives
in Higher Education KIRSTY COCHRANE *See page 54.*

Finnish Children's Literature RIITTA KUIVASMÄKI
1992 M 95-109 How the history of Finland, for six hundred years
dominated by Sweden but in the early nineteenth century annexed by
Russia, gave rise to a movement for Finnish identity that in its turn
fathered a literature for children that was mainly didactic. Largely concerned with the years up to 1917, the article covers the specialist
culture and moral teaching, the dependence on translation, the relationship with Swedish literature, poets, picture-book art; in a brief
summary of modern times: Tove Jansson, comic strip, critical journals.

How You Become a Children's Writer WIM HOFMAN
See page 39.

Reading New Books JAN CHAMBERS, PHIL CHAMBERS,
HELEN SIMMONS, MARGARET CLARK
1993 S 202-5 Roberto Piumini's *Mattie and Grandpa,* translated from
the Italian, reviewed from different viewpoints.
  1994 J 72-4 Maria Pia Alignani writes about Roberto Piumini's
work.

Madame de Ségur, Ideal Grandmother GWEN MARSH
1994 M 103-12 The life, career and influence of Mme la Comtesse de
Ségur, 'the most popular of all French writers for children', who dominated French children's literature in the nineteenth and early twentieth
centuries. A summary of later developments in France—the *bandes
dessinées,* translations into French, Père Castor and Babar—is
appended. Also discussed: Enid Blyton.

Tove Jansson THOMAS WARBURTON
1994 S 172-3 An eightieth-birthday tribute to the maker of Moomins
by her former editor at Schildts in Helsinki.

Crossing the Divide: Publishing Children's Books in the European Context KLAUS FLUGGE

1994 S 209-14   A Woodfield Lecture. A publisher laments British xenophobia, which leads to a one-way traffic in children's books. He compares Continental picture books with British, asks why British prizes exclude foreign nationals from consideration.

A THIMBLE PRESS CHRONOLOGY 1970-1994

The Thimble Press was set up by Aidan and Nancy Chambers in 1969 in order to publish the critical journal *Signal Approaches to Children's Books*. Separate publications developed from the writing in its pages. During the 1970s a sister journal, *Young Drama* edited by Aidan Chambers, was also produced, to attend to the allied subject of educational drama and theatre in education.

1970-1972

3 issues *Signal* per year
[1970's issues included the first articles by writers who would become regular contributors: Alan Tucker and Elaine Moss.]

1973-1975

3 issues *Signal*, 3 issues of *Young Drama* per year
[First *Signal* appearance of Hugh & Maureen Crago; of Robert Leeson; of Peter Hunt; of Charles Sarland]

1976

3 issues *Signal*, 3 issues *Young Drama*
Alan Tucker *Poetry Books for Children* A Signal Booklist

1977

3 issues *Signal*, 3 issues *Young Drama*
[Dorothy Butler's 'Cushla and Her Books' (full thesis published by Hodder & Stoughton, 1979); Aidan Chambers's 'The Reader in the Book' (receives first Children's Literature Association Criticism Award); first *Book Post* feature]

1978

3 issues *Signal*, 3 issues *Young Drama*
Lance Salway *Humorous Books for Children* A Signal Booklist

1979

3 issues *Signal*
[Enlarged format, with new cover, overseen by John Ryder & Michael Harvey; first Signal Poetry Award]
Jill Bennett *Learning to Read with Picture Books* A Signal Booklist
Alan Tucker *Poetry Books for Children* A Signal Booklist.
Second edition.

1980

3 issues *Signal*

[First *Signal* appearance of Margaret Meek; of Neil Philip]

Jill Bennett *Reaching Out: Stories for Readers of 6 to 8*
   A Signal Bookguide

Lance Salway *Humorous Books for Children* A Signal Booklist.
   Second edition.

1981

3 issues *Signal*

Elaine Moss *Picture Books for Young People 9-13* A Signal Bookguide

1982

3 issues *Signal*

Jill Bennett *Learning to Read with Picture Books* A Signal Bookguide.
   Second edition.

Jill Bennett *Reaching Out: Stories for Readers of 6 to 8*
   A Signal Bookguide. Reprint with updating inset.

Aidan Chambers *Plays for Young People to Read & Perform*
   A Signal Bookguide

Peggy Heeks *Ways of Knowing: Information Books for 7 to 9 Year Olds*
   A Signal Bookguide

1983

3 issues *Signal*

[Jane Doonan's first article for *Signal*]

Nancy Chambers, editor *The Signal Review of Children's Books 1*
   (books published during 1982)

Anne Wilson *Magical Thought in Creative Writing: The Distinctive
   Roles of Fantasy & Imagination in Fiction*

1984

3 issues *Signal*

Jill Bennett & Aidan Chambers *Poetry for Children* A Signal Bookguide

Nancy Chambers, editor *The Signal Review of Children's Books 2*
   (books published during 1983)

132

1985

3 issues *Signal*

Jill Bennett, *Learning to Read with Picture Books* A Signal Bookguide.
Third edition.

Nancy Chambers, editor *The Signal Selection of Children's Books 1984*

Elaine Moss *Picture Books for Young People 9-13* A Signal Bookguide.
Second edition.

1986

3 issues *Signal*

[Lissa Paul's first article for *Signal*]

Nancy Chambers, editor *The Signal Selection of Children's Books 1985*

Margery Fisher *Classics for Children & Young People* A Signal Bookguide

1987

3 issues *Signal*

[Peter Hollindale's first article for *Signal*]

Nancy Chambers, editor *Fiction 6 to 9: A Signal Bookguide*
(Contributors: Jill Bennett, Steve Bicknell, Elizabeth Hammill,
Susan Hood, Colin Mills, Elaine Moss, Mary Steele & Liz Tansley)

Nancy Chambers, editor *The Signal Selection of Children's Books 1986*

1988

3 issues *Signal*

Jill Bennett *Learning to Read with Picture Books* A Signal Bookguide.
Third edition with updating inset.

Nancy Chambers, editor *The Signal Selection of Children's Books 1987*
[this and the following two *Selection*s produced in association with
Westminster College, Oxford]

Peter Hollindale *Ideology and the Children's Book* (receives
Children's Literature Association Criticism Award)

Margaret Meek *How Texts Teach What Readers Learn*

Elaine Moss *Picture Books for Young People 9-13* A Signal Bookguide.
Second edition with updating inset.

Liz Waterland *Read with Me: An Apprenticeship Approach to Reading*
Revised second edition

1989

3 issues *Signal*

[First of special inserts on typography by John Ryder]

Nancy Chambers, editor *The Signal Selection of Children's Books 1988*

Tessa Rose Chester *Children's Books Research: A Practical Guide to Techniques & Sources*

Tessa Rose Chester *Sources of Information about Children's Books*

Mary Steele *Traditional Tales* A Signal Bookguide

1990

3 issues *Signal*

[First Patrick Hardy Lecture]

Nancy Chambers, editor *The Signal Selection of Children's Books 1989*

1991

3 issues *Signal*

Jill Bennett, *Learning to Read with Picture Books* A Signal Bookguide. Fourth edition.

Aidan Chambers *The Reading Environment*

1992

3 issues *Signal*

Brian Morse *Poetry Books for Children* A Signal Bookguide

Elaine Moss *Picture Books 9 to 13* A Signal Bookguide. Third edition.

1993

3 issues *Signal*

Aidan Chambers *Tell Me: Children, Reading and Talk*

Jane Doonan *Looking at Pictures in Picture Books*

1994

3 issues *Signal*

Liz Waterland *Not a Perfect Offering: A New School Year*

Details of *Signal*'s contents since 1994 and subsequent Thimble Press publications from the address on page 32.

INDEX

139

BACK ISSUES -- *Signal Approaches to Children's Books*

Published January, May, September ["73" = 1973]

[73J] [73S] [75J] [75M] [75S] [76J] [76M] [76S] [77J] [77M] [77S]

[78M] [78S] [79S] [80J] [80S] [81M] [81S] [82J] [82M] [82S] [83J]

[83M] [83S] [84J] [84M] [84S] [85J] [85M] [85S] [86J] [86S] [87J] [87M]

[87S] [88J] [88M] [88S] [89J] [89M] [89S] [90J] [90M] [90S]

Each of the above issues costs £2.50 ($4.50).

Please send issues circled. _____ [quantity] @ £2.50 ($4.50): _____

[91J] [91M] [91S] @ £2.90 ($5.25).. _____

[92J] [92M] [92S] [93J] [93M] [93S] @ £3.25 ($6)............. _____

[94J] [94M] [94S] [94J] [95M] [95S] @ £3.75 ($6.75)........_____

Payment enclosed...................._____

Overseas: Personal cheques accepted. All cheques to be drawn on bank in country of currency.
Photocopies of articles in out-of-print issues of SIGNAL are available. Details from address below.

The Thimble Press, Lockwood, Station Road, Woodchester, Stroud, Glos. GL5 5EQ U.K.

Please send the back issues indicated, post free, to:

NAME_____

ADDRESS_____

_____

_____post code_____